CENTRAL BANK DIGITAL CURRENCIES

T0292946

Also by Michael Lloyd and published by Agenda

British Business Banking: The Failure of Finance Provision for SMEs

CENTRAL BANK DIGITAL CURRENCIES

The Future of Money

MICHAEL LLOYD

agenda
publishing

First published in 2023 by Agenda Publishing

Agenda Publishing Limited
PO Box 185
Newcastle upon Tyne
NE20 2DH
www.agendapub.com

ISBN 978-1-78821-632-6

British Library Cataloguing-in-Publication Data
A catalogue record for this book is available from the British Library

Typeset by JS Typesetting Ltd, Porthcawl, Mid Glamorgan
Printed and bound in the UK by 4edge

CONTENTS

Introduction   1

1. Retail and wholesale CBDCs   9

   The changing environment for monetary payments   10
   The response of state regulators   13
   Current monetary system architecture and wholesale CBDCs   17
   Conclusion   20

2. Domestic monetary and legal implications   23

   Public money vs private money   24
   The problem of stablecoins   26
   The regulatory liability network   28
   The risks from the potential introduction of private money   30
   Implications of retail CBDCs for citizens   32
   Design options for CBDCs   34
   Consumer access to the CBDC   37
   Legal implications   39
   Monetary policy implications   43
   Cross-border payments   46
   Conclusion   48

3. Technology   51

   Central vs decentralized databases   51
   Distributed ledger technology   53
   Blockchain   57
   Commercial technology choices for central banks   60
   Smart contracts and programmability   62
   CBDC design options and technology platform choices   63

CONTENTS

Regulatory liability network   68
Cross-border payments   70
Conclusion   73

4. Impact on the commercial banking sector   75

    Commercial banking   75
    CBDCs and the commercial banking system   78
    Commercial bank reaction to CBDCs   81
    The role of credit card providers   87
    Other monetary system reform options   88
    Assessment of relative impacts   89
    Conclusion   92

5. The regional and international nexus   95

    The new global political economy   96
    China   101
    The United States   105
    EU digital euro   107
    Competing CBDCs   109
    Digital currency areas   110
    Cross-border wCBDC development   113
    A global digital reserve currency/unit of account   114
    Conclusion   116

6. The future of money: the next decade   119

    Money in the digital age   121
    Reforming domestic monetary systems   122
    The role of distributed ledger technology   123
    Political economy and society   124
    A global perspective   125

Appendix 1: Retail CBDC case studies   129
Appendix 2: Wholesale CBDC: cross-border examples   135
References   143
Index   155

INTRODUCTION

Money is almost as old as human civilization. All monetary tokens, bank notes for example, are a form of "IOU", expressing a social relation between creditor and debtor (Ingham 2004; Dodd 2014). The historical forms which money has taken have varied and the concept itself has been studied across many scientific and philosophical disciplines. The role and allocation of money in the multifarious forms of social, cultural, economic and political organization has always been crucial in influencing the structures and functioning of those organizational and societal forms.

It is broadly accepted, from historical and anthropological studies (Gayer 1937), that fiat money arose by the state issuing credit-tokens which were used by the state to purchase goods and services (including the military means to fight wars) and the state issued those credit-tokens in payment of taxes by citizens. In this manner the state's public monetary sphere subsumed the existing private credit networks, providing a guaranteed monetary anchor.

Money is not a physical object, but rather a system of recording account settlements denoted in a common *notional* unit of account. Money is not a commodity, whether it is physical money (cash) or digital money.

Luigi Einaudi (Gayer 1937: 265) indicates the historical evidence:

> Books and pamphlets and statutes of the ninth to the eighteenth century are unintelligible if one does not bear in mind the distinction between money of account or imaginary money and effective or coined money. Usually, the money of account was called libra, livre, lira. Men kept accounts, drew instruments of debt, sold and bought goods and securities and property rights in imaginary money, which they never saw. Coins had strange names, they poured into each country from all parts of the world, were gold and silver and half silver dresses, were minted at home or by foreign princes. They made no difference to people who continue to talk and negotiate and keep accounts in libras.

This account indicates the irrelevance of a "commodity-based" money and the necessity of having a "unit of account" based monetary system.

The cryptocurrency Bitcoin affords a modern demonstration of the inherent paradox in commodity-based money. It has a strictly controlled chain in supply (via hash-mining) and a maximum limit on creation over time (21 million coins). However, it has failed as a means of payment because of the extreme variability in its price relative to other commodities, including gold, and in its exchange rate with national currencies. The difference between a "Bitcoin system" and a "unit of account" settlement system is that the former neither provides a full balance sheet of debits and credits nor, crucially, a clearing system for netting balances. Its distributed ledger system simply records credit transfers, to ensure proof of payment and security, entirely within its closed system. Bitcoin does not have a unit of account monetary system function.

Jan Kregel explains the essence of the national central bank mediated system in providing the full accounting that Bitcoin lacks:

> If instead of individual accounts all participants in the system had accounts with a central bookkeeper who would keep track of the debits and credits in number units of account, the overall accounts would always balance, but there would still be individual imbalances that now could be automatically compensated by the central bookkeeper. If the bookkeeper is also the sovereign issuer of libra notes or mints gold libra coins they can arrange for the appropriate debts and credits in terms of notes or coins in the accounts of debtors and creditors. But since these are book entries, the notes and coins need not actually be transferred or even exist. In fact, they could be done away with (or buried in a vault or left under the sea ... in this social accounting money of account system, credits balances have value if they can be used to extinguish debts incurred in the production of goods and services.   (Kregel 2021: 13)

The central bookkeeper is, of course, the central bank.

Subsequent historical development led to the existing complex monetary system in a modern capitalist economy. Nonetheless, the creditor–debtor relationship is still at the heart of the economic development structures, allied to the monetary payment and settlement mechanism underlying economic exchange. It is important to recognize that money, in itself, has no intrinsic value. The monetary system serves the ultimate economic purpose of encouraging the deployment of the physical resources of land and human resources to hopefully productive ends.

Hence, underlying the monetary system are three acknowledged and essential functions: (1) as a medium of exchange (accepted payment for goods and services); (2) as a store of value (available future purchasing power); and (3) as a measure of value/a unit of account (against which goods and services are measured and deferred payment of debt is accepted). It is this last function on which the previous two functions rest and that acts as the bedrock of a modern capitalist economy. The state, in the form of a central bank, guarantees the currency that it issues and spends and accepts as payment of taxes, fines, and fees (so-called *fiat* money), and acts as the nation's bookkeeper, providing settlement of debts and credits.

Currently, commercial banks create loans to private citizens and companies which the central bank matches with reserves for the banks. Bank accounts are then used to facilitate payments, using this private money guaranteed by the central bank, issued to the regulated banking sector.

The government also has an account with the central bank, which it uses to pay for its expenditure on goods and services, and also uniquely, issues further interest-bearing sovereign debt as required. This debt may be purchased by the private sector, and any surplus is purchased by the central bank. In this manner, providing there is sufficient confidence in the fiat currency as a measure of value, and the probity and stability of the commercial banks is established, the economic and social functionality of the country is maintained.

The central bank provides the anchor for the modern monetary system, with additional support to the private financial system being provided by arrangements, such as prudential financial regulation (including Basel international regulation on banks' holdings of tiered equity capital) and deposit insurance to protect retail consumers.

Other private forms of money (IOUs) can and do exist, but they are unlikely to be widely accepted, as currently is the case with "stablecoins", even though these crypto-assets are linked to the value of a fiat currency, like the US dollar. In guaranteeing a fiat currency, the role of the central bank is crucial, as the financial institution that is a country's monopoly banknote issuer, manages the domestic money supply, sets interest rates, and acts as the "lender of last resort" to commercial banks. The central bank also serves as a clearing house for the final settlement of payments – it is the banker's bank. Many central banks also have supervisory and regulatory powers to ensure the solvency of commercial banks and the wider financial system, for instance, the Bank of England's Prudential Regulation Authority (PRA).

However, the advent of private digital currencies (so-called "cryptocurrencies") may in future threaten the stability of the current monetary system, based on fiat currencies. This potential has awakened central bank interest in issuing a retail digital currency, and in improving the efficacy of cross-border payment via extension of the existing wholesale digital currency system. Retail digital currencies issued directly to individual citizens, either to accompany, or potentially to replace, paper currencies and coinage are being considered by central banks. The decline of the use of cash in developed countries (and some developing countries) has been another motivating factor in considering the introduction of retail digital currencies. As research by the Bank of International Settlements (BIS) – an international forum for monetary policy discussions and facilitating financial transactions for central banks – states:

> In jurisdictions where access to cash is in decline, there is a danger that households and businesses will no longer have access to risk-free central bank money. Some central banks consider it an obligation to provide public access and that this access could be crucial for confidence in a currency. A CBDC could act like a 'digital banknote' and could fulfil this obligation.   (Chen *et al.* 2021: 66)

It is unsurprising that, in our increasingly digitalized society, the creation of central bank electronic money issued directly to the general public is being actively considered. The concept of a "central bank digital currency" (CBDC) was proposed decades ago by Nobel Laureate James Tobin (Auer 2020). However, discussion of CBDCs has increased noticeably since 2016 not least within the central banking fraternity itself and within several national governments. These discussions have been precipitated by the rapid expansion of private digital currencies, especially stablecoins, whose value is linked to fiat currencies, often the US dollar.

Research into the potential of central banks establishing their own retail digital currencies, complementing private retail payment systems, is being actively pursued by around 90 per cent of central banks across the world (Kosse & Mattei 2021). The detailed research involves technical and economic considerations, involving assessment of the implications for national monetary policy and the commercial banking sector. However, adoption of a CBDC will generate a variety of impacts on commercial banks and on the general public.

Retail CBDCs, with a direct relationship between the central bank and the public, would be a major step forward in the increasingly digital economy. The structure of political economy may be significantly altered as a result. The changes will make transparent the key issues concerning credit and money in society – that is the importance of maintaining trust between debtor and creditor, and the key role of central banks in providing citizens' ultimate trust in the probity and finality of financial payments in national and other wider regional jurisdictions. Any alteration to the current monetary system arrangements will require the maintenance of public confidence.

To date, only four central banks, those of China, Nigeria, the East Caribbean Currency Union, and the Bahamas, have launched and are actively piloting or operating their retail CBDCs. The Swedish Riksbank has pursued a private retail CBDC "proof of concept", and many other central banks are working on both retail and wholesale CBDCs, either individually or in collaboration. For developing countries, a major objective of the CBDC is to widen access to banking services, given that few people in developing countries have conventional bank accounts, although many more do have smartphones, which are being used as electronic payment instruments, in addition to payment cards.

For the developed world, the two chief motivations for introducing retail CBDCs are firstly, the need to counter the potential danger to financial stability of unregulated cryptocurrencies and the proliferation of stablecoins, and secondly, the need to adjust to the decline in the use of cash and the increasing use of smartphones for payment, which offers the potential for digital payments innovation by central banks. For China, it has been the fact that 94 per cent of mobile retail payments were accounted for by the commercial payment providers Alipay and Tencent (Engen 2022). Other factors include the high costs to merchants of debit and credit cards, despite technological advances, and the view that commercial banks have been slow to innovate and conservative in their responses to challenges from new private payment service providers.

Digital money does already exist, but its disbursement is restricted to regulated financial institutions, primarily commercial banks, whose customer interface is with these banks' private money. Retail CBDCs modify this conventional two-tier monetary system by making central bank digital money directly available to the general public, in the same way that cash is a direct claim on the central bank.

The first incarnation of a retail CBDC was launched in Finland in 1992, with the Avant smart card system (Grym 2020). The Revolut prepaid card is a modern, updated digital version of the same idea (Revolut 2020). Interestingly, the Avant card was designated as "e-money", and fell within the EU's e-money Directive, which means "electronically, including magnetically, stored monetary value as represented by a claim on the issuer which is issued on receipt of funds for the purpose of making payment transactions, and which is accepted by a natural or legal person other than the electronic money issuer" (Grym 2020: 15). Specifically, there was no credit risk involved, any payment was direct and complete. However, the e-money issued on the card had to be accepted as payment by someone other than the issuer. The lack of this demand was the problem that led to the demise of Avant, although there are some lessons to be learned from the (failed) experiment. Demand for a retail CBDC from the general public, and its acceptability by merchants, will need to be demonstrated. The advantage of CBDCs, as with the Avant card, is the absence of credit risk. Once the digital money stored on the card was spent, it was extinguished.

An attribute of retail CBDCs is the absence of credit risk for payment system participants, as they are a direct claim on the central bank and its balance sheet. A retail CBDC is the digital equivalent of cash – although unlike cash it is not anonymous – provided by the central bank. All other forms of central bank digital money currently in use are private money and represent a claim on an intermediary, such as a commercial bank. When the central bank issues its digital retail money directly to individual citizens and non-financial companies, it will represent a potential revolutionary change.

Turning to wider transnational implications of CBDCs, an increasing number of central banks are exploring the issuance and use of their fiat currencies in digital form – known as *wholesale* CBDCs – for cross-border financial transfers. This development has been stimulated by concerns for global financial stability at the prospect of unregulated stablecoins being used for cross-border financial transactions. Such a private money development will have uncertain implications for the regional and global financing of trade and other international transactions (commercial and personal). However, on the other hand there is also concern about the impact of the use of CBDCs, such as China's digital yuan, for this purpose. Chapter 5 sets out the issues raised to date, especially in the United States, relating to the development and extended use of China's digital yuan (e-CNY) for international trade. Clearly, realizing the full potential of CBDCs in increasing efficiency of cross-border payments will require international collaboration. The technical developments required are already being discussed and tested within the BIS's "m-CBDC Bridge" project involving countries including China. Sister projects, Project Dunbar, involving Australia and South Africa, and Project Helvetia involving the Swiss and French central banks are now reporting. The m-CBDC Bridge is a prototyping project and is perhaps the most important of the various regional wholesale CBDC projects, exploring the feasibility of expanding the national real time gross settlement (RTGS) systems in a cross-border, multicurrency environment.

Notwithstanding the uncertainties inherent in the on-going development of central banks' thinking on the issues, this book will examine the implications of the likely move to both retail and wholesale CBDCs, in the coming decade and beyond. It will focus on three main aspects: first, the nature of the introduction of retail CBDCs, which will have ramifications for monetary systems and the operation of monetary policy, for the operations of the commercial banking sector, and, not least, for its socio-economic impacts on citizens and the overall political economy; second, it will consider the various retail CBDC models and the technological options available for the establishment and operation of CBDCs; and third, it will investigate the international aspects of CBDCs, particularly in terms of the future potential for cross-border trade and financial transactions, involving wholesale CBDCs, including the potential development of large digital currency areas.

The book will examine the motivations of central banks in responding to the technological innovation and business development of new payment-providers, cryptocurrencies and, especially, stablecoins, alongside a detailed exploration of their approaches in the light of the current lack of comprehensive and consistent regulation of crypto-assets and exchanges. The following chapters will explore the current positioning of central banks in considering, researching, developing and implementing CBDCs; survey the contemporary monetary landscape, including the domestic monetary and legal implications of the technical CBDC model options being considered; examine the underlying selection of database technologies available and being considered by central banks; assess the impact of CBDCs on the commercial banking and financial sector and on intra-regional, cross-border trading and the wider international financial system; and, finally, it will consider the political economic impacts of CBDC and the implications for the future of money.

1
RETAIL AND WHOLESALE CBDCS

Central banks are actively involved in the research, development and piloting of retail digital currencies. The factors stimulating this active interest are several: (1) the decreasing use of cash for transaction purposes, especially in developed countries; (2) the increasing use of smartphone utilization in developed countries; (3) the absence, in less developed countries, of wide access to formal banking arrangements combined with the widespread availability of smartphones; (4) the availability of emerging digital information and communications technologies, driving a global digital age; and (5) a potential enhanced ability to target central bank monetary policy directly at individual consumer spending. There is also an urgency for central banks to explore wholesale cross-border CBDCs, given central banks' desire to maintain international financial stability. These various concerns are seen by central banks, and by governments, as requiring a defence of fiat currencies, the crucial trust-anchor role of central banks, and monetary/financial stability, within monetary jurisdictions (BIS 2021).

Central banks are especially concerned with the problems and risks associated with private international cross-border payments, and the opportunities presented for establishing wholesale CBDCs for cross-border financial transfers. Currently some 92 central banks around the world are participating in the various worldwide projects. For example, an April 2021 stock-take of central bank research and design efforts finds that out of 47 current retail CBDC projects, 11 are in addition exploring or piloting single national currency and multi-currency wholesale CBDCs in cross-border environments (Auer & Böhme 2021). Some jurisdictions such as The Bahamas, Nigeria and China, have launched their CBDCs. The cross-border dimension is being taken seriously by the G20 Road Map (FSB 2022) and being followed up by the BIS, given the potential for global trade instability of an extended use of stable-coins for this purpose. Several of these cross-border projects are discussed throughout this book and are detailed in the Appendices.

The salient features of the current monetary payments scene as it is evolving in digital forms are also explored, including the limited regulatory response of the state in most countries, and the general response of central banks, with several examples of CBDC approaches, within and across jurisdictions.

The changing environment for monetary payments

Over the past decade, the advent of improved, fast electronic transfer has led to an expansion of alternative financial payment providers offering rapid payment services as replacements for traditional banks' payment services (Lloyd 2021). Although "alternative finance" for business has achieved modest growth during the past few years, it still has a long way to go: "[i]ts share was around only 1.5–2 per cent of total lending to all UK non-financial businesses in 2018" (Lloyd 2021: 94). However, distributed ledger technology (DLT) and blockchain technology have provided opportunities for the rapid proliferation of cryptocurrencies, especially stablecoins, to facilitate financial transactions.

It is perhaps not surprising that concerns about "Big Tech" companies surfaced first in China. China is the world's leading country in terms of smartphone payments and its technology. This is largely thanks to mobile technology payment platforms, such as Alibaba's Alipay and Tencent's WeChat Pay, which allow users to make purchases in stores, pay bills and transfer funds to other individuals through digital wallets. According to a PricewaterhouseCooper's study (PwC 2019) 86 per cent of people in China used mobile payment platforms to make purchases in 2019. This was well ahead of Thailand, which had the second-highest percentage of mobile payments users (67 per cent) and more than twice the global average (34 per cent). According to data from the Peoples Bank of China (PBOC), the amount of money that changed hands in China via mobile payments grew from CNY11.7 trillion (US$1.9 trillion) in 2013 to a staggering CNY347.1 trillion (US$51.8 trillion) in 2019 (Daxue Consulting 2022).

The Chinese government has been concerned that the two tech giants, Alibaba and Tencent were not only dominating mobile payments but were also making substantial profits from their 20 per cent commission charge, at the same time as shifting the cost of customer default on to the Chinese commercial banks involved (Bloomberg Intelligence 2021). State regulatory action has been taken against both companies, but it has also prompted (see below) the initiative for the PBOC to launch its own digital currency for mobile payments.

However, across the developed world, there has been an increase in the development of private fast-payment platforms, which have proliferated since the development of cryptocurrencies, and especially since the advent of stablecoins. Even more concerning, for all countries, was the intention of Meta (then Facebook) to introduce its own stablecoin cryptocurrency. The initial proposed stablecoin, Libra, was intended to be linked to a basket of fiat currencies, including the dollar and the euro. This proposal was later abandoned in favour of a modified version (Diem) that was linked to the US dollar only. However, rather than launching Diem directly, instead, a modest initiative was launched in the form of a limited Novi wallet. This pilot programme enabled users to send and receive money "instantly, securely, and with no fees" using the Paxos stablecoin, in partnership with Coinbase, one of the major cryptoexchanges facilitating transactions. Even then, only a select number of users living in the US and Guatemala were permitted to use Novi.

The apprehension exhibited by many governments and regulators around the world about the proposed introduction of a Meta/Facebook stablecoin – given the 2.9 billion global users of Meta/Facebook – indicated that a Diem stablecoin would not be a welcome innovation. The response to this criticism, combined with other public bodies' concerns about Facebook's operations and dominance, led Meta in early 2022 to abandon Diem. No reasons have been given for its demise.

The ostensible aims of all the plethora of private fast-payment systems, whether or not based on cryptocurrencies or on stablecoins, are to reduce transaction fees, speed cross-border payments, and improve access to the millions of unbanked people across the world. However, some of the barriers the cryptocurrencies are supposed to overcome relate as much to the security checks that ensure legal compliance with anti-money-laundering requirements than to technological barriers. Nor is technology the only barrier to enabling the currently unbanked to open bank accounts; poverty incomes are not seen as warranting bank accounts. The US has a specific problem in not having a fast public banking payments system, such as the CHAPS and BACS systems in the UK or SEPA/SCT in the EU, although the US is now introducing "FedNow", which is set to go live in 2023. These systems, and others across several jurisdictions, are to be improved further in line with the new international standard messaging system ISO 20022, an ISO standard for electronic data interchange between financial institutions (see Chapter 4).

Nonetheless, cryptocurrencies continue to proliferate (McDonald 2021), including ones with grandiose claims such as World Coin, emanating from Silicon Valley, which proposes to be offered free to anyone in the world (Hypebeast 2021: 1). It is estimated that 300 million people across the world, 3.9 per cent of the global population (Triple A 2021), are in possession of some amount of the various cryptocurrencies now available. However, the ownership is likely to be skewed. In the case of Bitcoin (essentially now a store of value rather than widely used for payments, as originally envisaged), 70 per cent is owned by around 2 per cent of investors (Schultze-Kraft 2021).

It is not Bitcoin which concerns central banks. To understand the concern of the central banks it is worth looking briefly at three of the many stablecoin cryptocurrencies, all of which are tied directly and at parity to the US dollar: Tether, the most widely traded stablecoin; PAX, probably the fastest growing stablecoin, and the one selected for Facebook's piloting of Novi, as indicated above; and the BUSD stablecoin, which claims to be the "world's leading digital dollar stablecoin".

Transactions made in Tether have been reflected in its growth in assets from $3 billion in March 2020 to $69 billion in October 2021. According to Kaiko:

> Nearly 50 per cent of all Bitcoin trades are executed using Tether, which today is the most structurally critical stablecoin in the industry. Approximately $100 billion in Tether trade volume happens every day across dozens of exchanges and throughout 2021 regulators finally started paying attention, especially in the United States. The biggest focus was on the controversial makeup of Tether's reserves, although Circle's USDC also faced scrutiny.   (Kaiko 2021: section 9)

Not surprisingly this substantial growth in trading activity and assets has attracted attention from US regulators.

In February 2021, the New York Attorney General (NYAG), Letitia James, reached an $18.5 million settlement in its fraud case against the cryptocurrency exchange Bitfinex and its affiliated entity, stablecoin issuer, Tether. According to the NYAG, Tether's previous assurances about its reserve backing were deliberately deceptive. "In the face of persistent questions about whether the company actually held sufficient funds, Tether published a self-proclaimed 'verification' of its cash reserves, in 2017, that it characterized as 'a good faith effort on our behalf to provide an interim analysis of our cash position'", NYAG stated in a press release accompanying the announcement of the settlement. "In reality, however, the cash ostensibly backing tethers had only been placed in Tether's account as of the very morning of the company's 'verification'" (James 2021, no page).

In October 2021 the Commodities Future Trading Commission (CFTC) reached a settlement with Tether, which included a $41 million fine (Bitfinex, linked to Tether, was also fined $1.5 million). According to the CFTC, Tether's stablecoin was not fully backed by dollars. Moreover, Tether had "at least 29 [banking] arrangements that were not documented through any agreement or contract" (CTFC 2021).

So far PAX and the BUSD coin appear to be working with US regulators. This is because Paxos, the issuing company of both coins, is one of the two companies in the world (the other is Gemini) issuing regulated dollar-backed stablecoins. PAX and BUSD, are both issued by the Paxos Trust Company regulated by the New York State Department of Financial Services (NYDFS). Trusts are required by law to have their products and services approved and supervised by NYDFS.

The crucial difference between the Paxos and Tether companies is evidenced by the proportion of reserves each held in cash: 96 per cent in the case of Paxos and 3 per cent in the case of Tether.

However, the issues raised by stablecoin cryptocurrencies – the probity and resilience of some of the companies that issue them and the exchanges (often linked with the issuing companies) who facilitate the trading in these currencies and between them – are not the only problem. Rather is it the wider challenge to governments and central banks issuing fiat currency, and the public trust secured by central banks in those countries (absenting the, relatively infrequent, collapse of public trust in some countries). It is this latter concern with maintaining public trust, which is exercising the minds of central bankers around the world, with the constraint that central banks do not want to stifle private company technological innovation in the area of fast-payment systems. The innovative development of distributed ledger technology is a prime example here. Before looking at the response of central banks, it is worth considering the potential actions of state regulators in relation to the significant threat posed by stablecoins.

The response of state regulators

Whether or not there are specific instances of malpractice or corruption on the part of specific cryptocurrency companies and joint ventures with cryptoexchanges, there is the wider question as to whether the current cryptocurrency ecosystem is unstable in financial terms and therefore open to serious malfeasance. Although, little *general* regulation of cryptocurrencies has been enacted, China being a partial exception, most developed countries are contemplating regulatory action, either via existing regulators or by enacting specific regulation and establishing specific regulatory agencies for cryptocurrencies. The varied patchwork of legal regulation, taxation and regulatory action impacting on cryptocurrencies illustrates how jurisdictions are moving in these areas at differing paces and in different ways.

The October 2021 (IMF 2021) Global Stability Report indicated its concern about the scale of the cryptocurrency problem for the global financial community and the lack of regulatory coordination across jurisdictions, creating "regulatory gaps, inconsistent regulatory treatment, and regulatory arbitrage". A further problem is that the headquarters of some US dollar-based stablecoins are located offshore, operating via unregulated offshore banks. Moreover, the IMF notes that:

> Crypto asset markets are growing rapidly. Crypto asset prices remain highly volatile. Furthermore, the volume of crypto asset transactions has reached macro-critical levels in some emerging markets, often as high as those of domestic equities. A sound regulatory framework for crypto assets, and decentralized finance markets more generally, must be a priority on the global policy agenda. This is particularly pressing for stable-coins, for which some business models have been subject to the risk of sudden and severe liquidity pressures. A regulatory level playing field is a key priority. (IMF 2021: ix)

The growth of stablecoins has caught regulators off guard. It is estimated that since 2020, the stablecoin sector has expanded by 500 per cent, rising from a total market capitalization of around $20 billion to over $125 billion (Jagarti 2021). Governments, central banks and stablecoin issuers and traders, not surprisingly, have differing views about regulation. The three likely approaches for regulating stablecoins appear to be either to regulate the issuers as banks, to regulate the use of stablecoins as tradeable assets/securities that are convertible into cash in the fiat currency used by the stablecoin issuer, *or* to regulate them less comprehensively than commercial banks (Zelmer & Kronick 2021).

The lack of a coordinated and effective international regulatory action has prompted central banks to make preparations for potential future launches of their own public versions of digital money for retail payments. The regulatory framework in most jurisdictions is unclear and confused. This is especially the case in federal or quasi-federal jurisdictions such as the United States and the European Union, with a multiplicity of federal and lower-level regulatory agencies and laws.

In the majority of jurisdictions, current cryptocurrencies are not recognized as legal tender. To date only El Salvador, in 2021, has made a cryptocurrency, Bitcoin, legal tender. Notwithstanding some political pressure to follow suit, it seems highly unlikely that other Latin American jurisdictions will follow El Salvador's lead. Moreover, as there is a finite stock of Bitcoin to be hash-mined (21 million), it is more like a commodity (like gold) than a currency, it lacks scalability and has privileged access, and it may eventually be used as a store of value (currently it fluctuates widely), rather than as a medium of exchange. Perhaps most importantly, it will not be a universally accepted unit of account.

Most jurisdictions regard cryptocurrencies as securities, property, or an asset, and therefore are potentially (and in many cases actually) subject to taxation. The problem is that their decentralization, combined with the pseudonymity of transactions, means that the state is reliant on the self-reporting of capital gains, interest and profits. Any action taken by the authorities, such as the Securities and Exchange Commission (SEC) in the US, is likely to entail some form of legalized central registration, if tax avoidance is to be curbed.

The US importantly lacks a coordinated regulatory response, despite the prevalence of the circulation and use of cryptocurrencies within its overall jurisdiction. The SEC views a cryptocurrency as a security, whereas the Commodity Futures Trading Commission (CFTC) defines Bitcoin as a commodity, and the Treasury regards it as currency, although not as legal tender in the US. Cryptocurrency exchanges (such as Binance and Coinbase) fall within the regulatory scope of the Bank Secrecy Act and must register with the Financial Crimes Enforcement Network. They are also required to comply strictly with international (IMF) anti-money-laundering and combatting the financing of terrorism obligations. The Internal Revenue Service classifies cryptocurrencies as property for federal income tax purposes and states may also bring legal actions against the issuers of cryptocurrencies. The SEC is also investigating the leading digital currency exchange Coinbase Global Inc., in an attempt to provide further regulatory clarity as to whether or not most cryptocurrencies are, in practice, securities and should be regulated as investment assets.

The US President's Working Group has issued a report (US Treasury 2021) recommending legislation to regulate stablecoins, at the same time as Congress is interrogating stablecoin companies and crypto-asset exchanges, in preparation for regulatory action:

> The House of Representative Financial Services Committee convened in a virtual hearing in February 2022 to discuss the report on the financial risks of stablecoins and other digital assets. Nellie Liang, the Treasury Department's Under Secretary for Domestic Finance, joined the hearing to present the report's findings and emphasized the need for lawmakers to introduce some kind of legal framework for stablecoins and other novel types of digital assets. "There is flexibility within the [insured depository institution] framework to not focus on the credit risk of making loans," Liang said, referring to the working group's recommendations. "Stablecoin issuers do not make loans. They don't engage in fractional reserve banking. But they do have payments, and there are operational and convertibility risks that are associated with that. (US House of Representatives Financial Services Committee 2022)

Whether this "concession" will satisfy the US sceptics, including in Congress, calling for minimal regulation of stablecoins is not clear (Atkins & Noreika 2022). In September 2020, the European Commission proposed the Markets in Crypto-Assets Regulation (MICA). A framework that will attempt to increase consumer protections by establishing clear crypto-industry rules of conduct, and to introduce new licensing requirements. Currently, the proposed Regulation is going through its first readings in the Council and the European Parliament. As of November 2021, the European Council issued the MICA negotiating mandate with the European Parliament (European Council 2021). In March 2022, the European Parliament adopted its negotiating mandate for the "trilogue" between the Council, Parliament and European Commission to begin, as the prelude to the eventual enactment of the Directive legislation. The scope of the regulation is considerable, however it does not apply to any of the DLTs underlying cryptocurrencies, nor to CBDCs issued by member states. What it does cover are private cryptocurrencies including tokens of various kinds appertaining to cryptocurrencies.

The proposed EU regulation subjects cryptocurrency exchanges, generically called "crypto asset services", to consumer protection, transparency and governance standards, thereby protecting consumer funds against any malfunctions that are within the responsibility of the crypto-exchanges. The regulatory reach over stablecoins is considerable, although not surprising, given the challenges they pose to fiat currencies. The other major focus of the regulation is on cryptocurrency exchanges where stablecoins are traded, and interest is paid on the stablecoin accounts held in the exchanges. This interest will be prohibited by the proposed regulation, thus protecting the European banking sector.

Stablecoins will need to be authorized by national regulatory institutions to be traded within the EU including stablecoins already in circulation. Here, the regulation follows a similar model to that of EU competition law enforcement, in that it will primarily be enforced by national regulatory authorities designated by the member states. Cryptocurrency projects and organizations will have to be registered as legal entities in at least one of the member states. However, there will also be, as with EU banking, regulation at EU level. Supervisory powers will be given to the European Banking Authority and the European Securities and Markets Authority. The European Central Bank will be involved in providing a non-binding opinion on stablecoins, in advance of their approval.

China has already taken a tough line on Bitcoin mining, introducing in 2021 a countrywide blanket-ban on all crypto transactions, including stablecoins and hash-mining. Ten agencies, including the central bank, financial, securities and foreign exchange regulators work together to eliminate "illegal" cryptocurrency activity. China's National Development and Reform Commission has stated it will cut off financial support and the supply of electricity for the extremely energy-intensive hash-mining for Bitcoin. The People's Bank of China (PBOC) has banned the circulation of cryptocurrencies and overseas exchanges are barred from providing services to China-based investors. It has also barred financial institutions, payment companies and internet firms from facilitating cryptocurrency trading nationally. Binance, the world's biggest crypto-exchange, has been blocked from operating in China since 2017. Other crypto-exchanges, OKEx and Huobi, which both originated in China, are now based overseas. Their position is unclear.

The UK regards investments in cryptocurrencies, including stablecoins, as securities *or* property assets, so therefore taxable under capital gains. However, it also classifies crypto-assets into two other categories: e-money tokens, which are subject to regulation under the Electronic Money Regulations, and unregulated tokens, namely utility tokens used to access a service or exchange tokens, such as Bitcoin, that can be used for payment. Unfortunately, it is these unregulated tokens that represent the bulk of crypto-asset activity in the UK, and hence, evade regulatory control. They pose a major problem for the Financial Conduct Authority (FCA), the main regulatory agency involved in consumer investment protection.

According to the FCA, as many as 2.3 million UK consumers hold crypto-assets, notwithstanding their high volatility and their association with money-laundering and other financial crime (FCA 2021). Since January 2020, under the existing Money Laundering Regulations, businesses defining themselves as crypto-businesses have been required to register with the FCA.

France has taken a softer line in the regulation of crypto-assets. Binance has received regulatory approval to establish its European headquarters in France (Liao 2022). Binance claimed to have 85 million users in 2020. However, other sources suggest lower figures, "as of October 2021, according to an estimate, there are 28.6 million Binance users" (McGovern 2022). It has invested €100 million in its structure and services.

Nonetheless, the situation globally is that China and India have both now banned trading in all cryptocurrencies (although it is not clear how rigorously such an outright ban can be regulated). Hence, even if the developed country jurisdictions permit some regulated usage of stablecoins, there will be a significantly limited global market for these private currencies. How this will be resolved is not yet clear. What is perhaps clearer is that central banks – although in some countries, such as the UK, they do have a regulatory input – have not simply waited for regulators to act. Their concerns are with domestic and global financial stability in a rapidly innovating digital world.

Current monetary system architecture and wholesale CBDCs

It is important to recognize that digital currencies have been around for some time. However, the issuance of electronic money has been *restricted*, to banks and certain other privileged or regulated financial intermediaries. Effectively, this system may be referred to as a *wholesale digital currency system*. In this

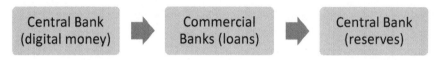

Figure 1.1 Wholesale CBDC

model the only direct recipients of central bank digital money are commercial banks (and a few other privileged financial institutions). The non-financial corporate sector and the general public participate in the system only *indirectly*. The essence of the current *wholesale* digital currency system may be summarily illustrated in Figure 1.1. This simplified relationship indicates that digital money is created, indirectly in a wholesale system, as private money within commercial banks as they issue loans (assets on their balance sheets by deposit liabilities) which are then matched by equivalent central bank reserves (liabilities on its balance sheet).

What is now being proposed is a *retail* digital money system in which non-financial businesses and individual citizens will also have access to, and be able to hold, digital currency/money issued to them directly by the central bank. This establishes a direct relationship between the citizen and the central bank, rather than access via commercial bank private money, backed by central bank money. The digital money is equivalent to physical cash, and may be used by economic actors for payments, although it is not the same as cash. The broad design for the issuance of digital money to citizens by the central bank may be illustrated by two simplified relationships shown in Figure 1.2, which shows two possible modes (account-based and token-based) of central bank digital money going directly to all economic actors, not simply commercial banks.

First, it is worth clarifying the impact of any introduction of retail CBDCs on the use of cash. The use of cash for payment has been declining in many countries for a number of years. The impact of Covid-19, and the associated concerns around handling cash in terms of potential infection contagion (possibly exaggerated), has accelerated this trend. However, there is evidence from the UK that relative to GDP cash usage has increased in the so-called "grey economy", accompanying the increased proportion of self-employment and VAT avoidance (Ashworth & Goodhart 2020).

Figure 1.2 Retail CBDC (account-based and token-based)

Essentially, digital currency may be seen as the electronic form of cash, in other words a substitute for cash with the same direct link between the citizen and the central bank. The well-known central bank "promise to pay the bearer of" printed on banknotes will still be honoured with their digital form. However, the cryptographic control over digital currency, to prevent double spending, will make tax avoidance easier to track. However, although digital currencies are substitutes for cash, albeit without the anonymity of physical cash, it is likely that cash will remain in circulation, and be held by citizens, for many years to come, even if in various countries cash may, eventually, cease to be used. For instance, in Sweden (apparently unlike the UK), it is estimated that less than 10 per cent of payment transactions currently involve cash.

However, and perhaps especially for the elderly or those unable to access bank accounts, the attachment to the use of cash will remain. Nor will it be necessary, for a considerable number of years to remove the ability to use cash for payment settlement, either banknotes or larger coin denominations. Digital money and physical cash may co-exist harmoniously for a number of years. ATMs (automatic teller machines) will probably continue to reduce in number, as is already happening, but they will not disappear for some time. Indeed, at the moment, not one central bank has proposed eliminating cash.

There are two counterposed delivery variants of a retail CBDC. The first is a direct, possibly, token-based delivery model in which a central bank issues digital token substitutes for cash in the wallets (digital) of individuals and companies, which can either be stored at commercial banks or kept separately, as in a smartphone wallet. Here there will need to be secure, digital identification for the individual to access and utilize the digital money sent to them, and a listing of the tokens and their values by banks. The customer will have a direct claim on the central bank. The second is an indirect accounts-based delivery model in which the central bank issues money into the customer's digital money account at the commercial bank, which then adjusts the customer's account balances as the central bank digital money is received and spent, in the same manner as it does with the separate private money accounts at the bank. In this variant the customer will not have a direct claim on the central bank, only on the commercial bank.

Other model designs fall in-between these two extremes and the full range of retail CBDC model design options will be outlined and considered in Chapter 2. However, in all models the *management* of the digital money accounts will be done by the commercial banks or by the individual in the case of smartphone wallets. In practice, as will be argued in later chapters, central banks are likely to take a gradualist approach and use a retail CBDC model design that involves minimal operational change for both commercial banks and their customers, and their perception of the existing monetary system. By managing the introduction of CBDCs in this manner the aim would be to gain a readier acceptance of the change than with a more radical approach.

Notwithstanding the concentration of most current political and academic discussions of CBDCs on retail CBDCs, there is considerable interest from central banks, and the Bank of International Settlements (Kosse & Mattei 2022), in extending the current wholesale CBDCs to handle cross-border financial transfers, with priority given to three major BIS-led CBDC projects (see Appendix 1 for the various different projects currently underway in retail and wholesale CBDCs). Although there is concern among central banks about the impact of stablecoin digital currencies in domestic financial markets, the potential for disruption of regional and international financial markets is more worrying for the central banks. The ability, therefore, to explore mechanisms to extend the domestic RTGS (real time gross settlement) systems in a cross-border context is now a priority and active area of interest (see also Chapter 5).

Conclusion

It is apparent that the increasing digitization of payments systems – especially by new entrants in the private sector, in competition with banks and traditional credit card company operations – has prompted central banks to actively explore the options for establishing domestic retail CBDCs and cross-border wholesale CBDCs. Moreover, there has been special concern about the advent of cryptocurrencies, including notably stablecoins, seeking to establish private fast payment channels. It is this unregulated private pathway that may, in the near future, challenge the existing public, fiat currency systems across currency areas, both within and between jurisdictions, that has encouraged the launching of the rapid array of CBDC projects.

The potential of stablecoins – and notable early fears about the potential of Facebook's now abandoned Diem – has already stimulated, across various national and currency area jurisdictions, the potential introduction of regulation affecting private cryptocurrencies and crypto-exchanges. The international approach to such regulation is variable as is its implementation The position the United States takes will be influential. So far it seems unlikely, given business and political pressures, that an outright ban on stablecoin will emerge. Opinion in the US from the banking sector (Baer 2021), including some in the Federal Reserve (Waller 2021), is distinctly cool about the desirability of a US CBDC, although research is being undertaken by the Federal Reserve in Boston and MIT (see Chapters 3 and 4).

For large commercial companies and the professional private investment sector stablecoins may well be used for payment purposes. It is also possible that regulation would permit investment in stablecoins as assets. The potential for coexistence rather than competition, between CBDCs and stablecoins in the payments area, is also under consideration in the US by Congress. Regulatory proposals to date include the EU's MICA legislative proposal and the US Presidential Working Group (PWG) recommendations. However, given the breadth and depth of CBDC exploration by the world's central banks it seems possible that in order to preserve their fiat currencies and the associated monetary stability and monetary policy control, regulation may be supplemented by the establishment of CBDCs in several countries. The current lack of international comprehensive and consistent regulation, together with other factors, has prompted central banks to try to ensure that, via CBDCs, the essential societal public trust provided by central banks is maintained.

CBDC development for cross-border payment purposes appears to be developing, at least initially, via the exploration of wholesale CBDC DLT approaches, as for instance with the Inthanon project of the Bank of Thailand, thus preserving the RTGS systems, currently operated domestically. The Inthanon project has been extended, via the Inthanon-LionRock project, and the prototyping of an even wider cross-border wholesale CBDC payments system is now being taken over by the BIS Multi-CBDC Bridge project, whose membership (including China) and project approach has been briefly described. Other projects are exploring CBDC cross-border payments.

The BIS is providing a strong impetus for this exploration (involved in three major projects), given major concerns about potential disruption of regional and international cross-border payments from any substantial establishment of private money channels via unregulated stablecoins in this cross-border financial transfer arena.

Notwithstanding the significant activism of central banks in exploring, and in some cases launching retail CBDCs, consideration by governments has been more limited, so far. As will be illustrated in future chapters various interest groups, such as commercial banks, technology companies, stablecoin issuers, and politicians across several countries, have differing opinions. Governments are obviously aware of their own central banks' activities in respect of CBDCs, and probably sometime in the relatively near future will have to start consultations on the issue, not the least because of the legal implications.

In the next chapter, the four main CBDC model design options and the various financial, monetary and economic implications, and potential impacts of CBDCs are explored.

2
DOMESTIC MONETARY AND LEGAL IMPLICATIONS

The suggested shift to a retail CBDC model involving digital money transfers to the corporate and personal (individual citizens) sectors will represent a crucial change in the monetary architecture serving retail payments and savings. The various monetary, financial, economic and legal implications of the approaches being explored for the potential issuance of CBDCs – some elements of which are being explored in the approaches taken in the various CBDC projects – will therefore need to be addressed.

The potential use of CBDCs in cross-border financial transfers will need to be examined by exploring the involvement of central banks' RTGS systems proposed use in this area, including how central banks are experimenting with its extension via wholesale CBDC structures, in a multi-currency environment in order to secure stability, security and control over a key element of the global financial and trading system (BIS 2022a).

The contentious possibility, raised by some commentators (Zellweger-Gutknecht 2021) of introducing monetary action aimed at directly controlling consumer expenditure will be discussed, in the context of the current complex of conventional, and what are now considered "unconventional", monetary policy instruments.

The importance of central bank money (fiat) money to the whole monetary system is difficult to overstate: it provides the central trust-anchor for the banking system and underpins the trust that citizens have in their currencies. Unless regulated, stablecoins, as a new digital source of private money, pose a potential threat to this fundamental role of the central bank. Although, private money exists in the current monetary system and is ubiquitous as commercial bank money, used by businesses and by the general public, its role is uniquely supported by the central bank. Commercial bank private money (in the form of deposits matching commercial bank loans, as assets), is matched one-to-one by the parallel reserves, created as liabilities at the central bank. These reserves are public money and serve to guarantee the private money created by the commercial banks. Unregulated stablecoins, on the other hand, are tied to the value of the various fiat currencies, but they are not matched by public money created by the relevant central banks as reserves. Neither are they able to provide the trusted settlement and clearing system offered by a well-performing central bank, utilizing the provision of a universally-accepted unit of account.

Public money vs private money: competition and cooperation

For some years, notwithstanding the global financial crisis, there has been a broad consensus between central banks and commercial banks concerning an acceptable balance between competition and cooperation in relation to payment systems. Central banks have provided the principal means of final settlement of transfers between commercial banks because central bank public money, fiat money, is the most liquid asset in any monetary jurisdiction and because the central bank is trusted. There is variation across central banks as to the partial use of other assets, including commercial bank private money – for instance, the Federal Reserve has a more flexible approach than the Bank of England (BIS 2003) – but the principal means of final settlement across the world remains central bank money, in a context of cooperation with commercial banks. As already noted, public awareness is limited, only the banknote exemplifies this trust (and liquidity) for the citizen. As the BIS report suggests, "[b]eing intrinsically worthless pieces of paper that everyone accepts from a stranger in exchange for valuable goods and services, banknotes testify to the presence of certain bonds of confidence that tie together the members of a society" (BIS 2003, no page).

Over the past decade, new internet-based payment providers have emerged to compete with the commercial banks, but have not, so far, seriously threatened the banks (Lloyd 2021: 94). This situation has not changed materially with the appearance of cryptocurrencies, even Bitcoin. But the emergence and rapid development of stablecoins is transforming the monetary system environment, and this competition is threatening the central bank clearance and settlement role. The challenge for stablecoin issuers, of course, is how to provide both liquidity and trust.

Notwithstanding, the crucial importance of central bank public money, commercial banks are the primary issuer of *private* money. Their liabilities (deposits, matching the provision of loans to businesses and to personal customers) represent 97 per cent of the stock of money created. However, there are, as indicated above, a large number of other payment mechanisms established by other institutions, including several new banks and now stablecoin issuers. Hence, there is increased and significant competition in the area of banking and payment systems, although none of the non-bank payment system providers have access to central bank reserves and none are involved in credit creation in the same manner as commercial banks, though they may offer loans.

Central bank and commercial bank money (plus the other issuers) *coexist* in a modern monetary economy. However, confidence and trust in a commercial bank's money rests on its ability to convert their liabilities either into another commercial bank's money indirectly, or eventually, directly into central bank money. Confidence in the central bank depends on its ability to maintain price stability, ensuring that the monetary system balance sheet is always balanced. This trust-anchor role represents the central bank's pursuit of the public interest in social and economic stability, a public good.

The fundamental issue for any payments system is how (final) settlement of the payment or any credit arrangement is to be made. A payment system may be defined, narrowly, as a set of instruments, procedures and rules to achieve settlement, such as in the transfer of funds from one commercial bank to another. The settlement of the payments between the banks will take place at the "settlement institution", the central bank, by the exchange of the liabilities of the central bank, reflected in the deposits of the commercial banks at the central bank. In this manner, the set of individual commercial banks' debits and credits are reconciled in the central bank's accounts. Deposits at the central bank and any liquidity credit extended by the central bank to the commercial banks are both accepted as money by all the participants in the settlement system (BIS 2003). This clearance and settlement system – with some minor variations regarding recognized financial intermediaries involved, beyond regulated commercial banks – represents the main form of monetary architecture across the world's developed economies.

From the viewpoint of the public, this symbiotic relationship between central bank public money and commercial bank private money goes unnoticed. The continuing financial stability of the monetary system ensures that they are content to operate with private commercial bank money – save, of course, for cash – except for extreme financial crises.

The private sector's innovative development of digitization has now reached a point where publicly available payment systems, involving stablecoins, exploiting blockchain and distributed ledger technology, may pose a threat to this financial stability. This situation, coupled with the decline in cash usage, has encouraged central banks to consider taking advantage of the same innovative digital technologies to transform the delivery of public money, both to the public via retail CBDCs and to develop new, improved and lower cost cross-border, multi-currency financial transfers via wholesale CBDCs.

The problem of stablecoins

In November 2021, the President's Working Group (PWG), together with the Federal Deposit Insurance Corporation (FDIC) and the Office of the Comptroller of the Currency (OCC), released a report on stablecoins. The report confined itself to prudential risks arising from the use of stablecoins as a means of payment; other wider risks, such as digital assets and digital asset trading exchanges, were not considered. The following extract sets out the report's approach:

> Legislation should address the risks outlined in this report by establishing an appropriate federal prudential framework for payment stablecoin arrangements. In particular, with respect to stablecoin issuers, legislation should provide for supervision on a consolidated basis; prudential standards; and, potentially, access to appropriate components of the federal safety net. To accomplish these objectives, legislation should limit stablecoin issuance, and related activities of redemption and maintenance of reserve assets, to entities that are insured depository institutions. The legislation would prohibit other entities from issuing payment stablecoins. Legislation should also ensure that supervisors have authority to implement standards to promote interoperability among stablecoins. Insured depository institutions include both state and federally chartered banks and savings associations, the deposits of which are covered, subject to legal limits, by deposit insurance, and which have access to emergency liquidity and Federal Reserve services.
>
> Like other insured depository institutions, insured depository institutions that issue stablecoins would be subject to supervision and regulation at the depository institution level by a federal banking agency and consolidated supervision and regulation by the Federal Reserve at the holding company level. The standards to which these institutions are subject include capital and liquidity standards that are designed to address safety and soundness and, for the largest banking organizations, also include enhanced prudential standards that address financial stability concerns. Under the Federal Deposit Insurance Act, insured depository institutions also are subject to a special resolution regime that enables the orderly resolution of failed insured depository institutions by, among other mechanisms, protecting customers' insured deposits, and according priority to deposit claims over those of general creditors, and limits any potential negative systemic impacts in the event of bank failure. (US Treasury 2021: 16)

Essentially, the report advocated bringing stablecoin issuers into the ambit of regulated financial intermediaries and commercial banks.

The response to the report has been mixed, including from the stablecoin and general crypto community, and among banks and academic commentators. Jeremy Allaire, co-founder and chairman of Circle, which manages USDC, the second largest stablecoin token responded positively, "This is huge progress in the acceptance of stablecoins and provides a path for their adoption" (1 November 2021, Twitter). Tether, the stablecoin market leader was also similarly positive in its response. It may be that this warm response reflects the view that the PWG's attention to stablecoins may "fend off" any tough action by regulators. Tether is already under scrutiny by regulators (the SEC), as is Circle.

A contrasting response has come from others in the crypto industry. Coin Center, a crypto think tank, and the Chamber of Digital Commerce, both argued that bringing stablecoins within the same regulatory ambit as commercial banks could stifle innovation and also ignored payment systems like PayPal, which would not be similarly treated. Perianne Boring, founder of the Chamber, said that, "We believe that regulators should allow the 'laboratories of democracy' – the states – to continue to innovate in this space, rather than imposing one size fits all federal mandates" (Handagama 2021). This statement indicates a tactic used by the crypto industry, to play off the individual states against the federal government. Another group of cryptocurrency issuers appeared to think that the PWG report was a positive result. These were the smaller subset of stablecoin issuers (sometimes referred to as "synthetic" or "algorithmic" stablecoins) that use other means to stabilize the price of the instrument or are convertible to assets other than the fiat currency. Their omission from the PWG report does not, however, mean that regulators, such as the SEC, would not take action against these stablecoin issuers.

The outcome of regulation in the US is likely to be less stringent than the PWG has suggested (Atkins & Noreika 2022). The issue raises a general problem with the regulation of stablecoins in that the aim of regulation is to mitigate systemic financial risks, and protect especially small retail customers, while enabling innovation, especially from new entrants to the sector. The potential inability for regulation to achieve this objective on a consistent basis over time, was one major reason why central banks began to explore retail CBDCs. The potential danger of the regulatory authorities tightly regulating stablecoins may have been one of the reasons for a consortium of banks,[1] to suggest the inclusion of (regulated) stablecoin issuance *within* a conceptual and technology framework that would include commercial banks and central banks, hence

---

1. Including Citi, OCBC Bank, Goldman Sachs, Barclays, BondeValue, Bank of America, Bank of New York, Payoneer, Paypal, Wells Fargo, SETL and Linklaters.

designating all public *and* private money issuance involved as being "sovereign money" (McLaughlin 2021).

The regulatory liability network

The innovative financial market infrastructure of a regulated liability network (RLN), proposed by the consortium of US commercial banks, contains a conceptual design structure in which regulated institutions – including central banks, commercial banks and e-money providers – would *tokenize*[2] their liabilities (DiCaprio & McLaughlin 2022). These liabilities will share one common characteristic: the promise to pay the customer, on demand, at equal value in fiat currency units. This characteristic means that the tokens would work with, rather than replace, existing legal instruments. The primary focus of the concept is that there should be a common settlement infrastructure, operated by the central bank, for the network of regulated entities.

Tokens would be issued by any of the three regulated institutions, not, as now, by the central bank alone, and would simply be representations of existing deposits and represent claims on the specific individual issuer. Digital wallets or accounts would only be available to clients/customers following strict "know your customer" (KYC) identity checks. Payment transfers between the participating institutions work by extinguishing liabilities of the sender and creating matching liabilities on the receiving side. Final settlement is achieved only via central bank liabilities in tokens between all participants. The RLN would be a new Financial Market Infrastructure (FMI), observing the Principles for Financial Market Infrastructure set by the BIS Committee for Payments and Market Infrastructures (CPMI 2012) and the International Organization of Securities Commissions (IOSCO). The system would be the application layer run on top of a modified distributed ledger database platform, in a decentralized fashion. The RLN would also be able to accommodate other assets, by the regulated entities, such as sovereign or corporate bonds.

This innovative conceptual design is presumably motivated by an assumption, on the part of the authors of the RLN proposal, that there is sufficient motivation in the US to support CBDCs, if a monetary formulation and technology framework can be established which provides a parallel and monetarily equal route for stablecoins. However, the proposal represents a major challenge to the existing basis of a single trust-anchor in monetary systems, namely the fiat currencies issued solely by a central bank. Although superficially similar to the current global monetary architecture of public and private institutions and

---

2. A token is a digital unit representing a financial asset.

balance sheets, the suggested approach appears to involve the adoption of a re-definition of sovereign money.

In the RLN design, digital money would be issued directly to the public by the private sector and not, as now by the state to regulated commercial banks, directly matched by central bank reserves (public money), and then on to the general public. It is correct to say that the final settlement would be achieved solely by the central bank in the system. However, the private currencies, issued by the regulated commercial banks and by stablecoin issuers, also regulated entities, would have equal status to central bank issued digital money. What is not clear is what constitutes the liabilities that are being transferred and what the assets on the stablecoin balance sheets are. Moreover, if as suggested settlement is only via the central bank, then what volume of settlement will be required? Insofar as only net settlements would be required – after settlement is also achieved between the other participants, as it is currently – this would be manageable.

Whether this involves a redefinition of sovereign money depends on the content of the regulation of stablecoin issuers. If these issuers are regulated in exactly the same way as commercial banks, then it is not clear if the proposal is radical in any way. All that will happen is that an increased number of commercial banks will have been created, which is useful in competition terms, but is not a revolutionary concept. It should also be noted that the proposal also requires a tokenized system, whereas the majority of central banks are, currently, not considering tokenized systems.

As the Citibank paper notes, to maintain financial systemic stability, all digital money must satisfy four essential requirements: it must (1) be regulated, (2) be redeemable at par value on demand, (3) be denominated in national currency units, and (4) represent an unambiguous legal claim on the regulated issuer. It is not clear whether for stablecoins this last condition will be met, although as suggested above, it will depend on the nature of the regulation imposed on the issuers. The Citibank proposal appears ambitious:

> DLT has the potential to represent multiple forms of digital value, we might go further and envision the creation of networks that tokenize regulated liabilities and regulated assets on the same chain. Such a network would be significantly different from today's siloed financial architecture – a regulated internet of value. This system would embody tokenized currencies, bonds, equities, trade instruments and other regulated financial instruments in an 'always on', programmable and global network.   (McLaughlin 2021)

Even if such a monetary architecture was found to be technologically feasible and practicable (see Chapter 3), it is not clear that the equality of privately issued digital money (stablecoins) with publicly issued fiat digital money would be acceptable to central banks and to governments, unless it was clear that the regulation imposed, especially in relation to the quality of the balance sheet assets and the capital adequacy ratios, are the same as for commercial banks. Considerable further clarification on these and other aspects of the proposal are required.

The risks from the potential introduction of private money

Currently, bank deposits are protected across the EU and in the UK with deposit insurance for each account holder, to the value of £85,000 in the UK and the euro equivalent sum. In the US, the Federal Deposit Insurance Corp (FDIC) guarantees deposits of up to $250,000 per person, per bank. If the means of payment were to be provided by private stablecoins such protection would not currently be covered. Not unlike in the parallel case of peer-to-peer (P2P) lending systems, such as Funding Circle, where the internet intermediary takes on the contractual task of directly linking borrowers and savers in return for fees and commissions, but the risk of default is taken on by the lenders/savers; the borrowers have no risk.

The nature of risks related to credit securities are influenced by technological innovation, but such risks of private money and other financial assets should be viewed, notwithstanding the technological context, as a legal one. It should be recalled that the last major, private technological innovation was in relation to the uncertain valuation of novel financial derivatives that led to the 2008 global financial crisis.

The US Federal Reserve Governor, C. J. Waller, in a speech in November 2021 (Waller 2021: no page), has suggested a less conventional form of regulation for stablecoin issuers. In fact, his lighter regulation would prevent stablecoin issuers from engaging in maturity transformation and offering credit to its customers. It is not clear how this would be viewed by the companies involved. Waller argues that:

> the regulatory and supervisory framework for payment stablecoins should address the specific risks that these arrangements pose – directly, fully, and narrowly. This means establishing safeguards around all of the key functions and activities of a stablecoin arrangement, including measures to ensure the stablecoin "reserve" is maintained as advertised. But it does not necessarily mean imposing the full banking rulebook, which is geared in part toward lending activities, not payments. If an entity were to issue stablecoin-linked liabilities as its sole activity; if it backed those liabilities only with very safe assets; if it

engaged in no maturity transformation and offered its customers no credit; and if it were subject to a full program of ongoing supervisory oversight, covering the full stablecoin arrangement, that might provide enough assurance for these arrangements to work.

[...] Policymakers will continue to work through these questions in the coming months, but in the process, we should not let the novelty of stablecoins muddy the waters. The United States has a long history of developing, refining, and integrating new payment technologies in ways that maintain the integrity of its financial institutions and its payment system. Stablecoins may be new, but their economics are far from it. We know how to make this kind of privately issued money safe and sound, and, in designing a program of regulation and supervision to do so, we have plenty of examples to draw on. In the interest of competition and of the consumers it benefits, we should get to work.

The most important risk, which Waller accepts, but downplays, is that of the scale of a dominant stablecoin issuer producing damaging network effects and exerting monopolistic power over the payments system. Waller argues that rapid scaling-up "is not a concern as long as there is sufficient competition within the stablecoin industry and from the existing banking system".

Given the rapid development of several "Big Tech" dominant transnational companies, such as Google, Facebook and Amazon, this appears to be somewhat complacent, especially given the initial fears among many central banks about the Libra/Diem stablecoin proposal of Meta/Facebook, given the global user penetration of Facebook. Although Meta/Facebook has abandoned the Diem development project, for reasons that *may* have little to do with the stablecoin project itself, there is every reason to expect another dominant player to emerge. Even if one does not emerge, the oligopolist structure of modern major commercial banking does not offer much comfort for the future for a stablecoin market. Moreover, at root, the position of Waller, and of several others, especially in the US, appears to be based on a belief that private money is either superior or equivalent to public money. Global monetary history confounds this view.

A more detailed analysis in a Federal Reserve working paper (Liao & Caramichael 2022) considers three markets for stablecoin use: digital asset trading, intra-company trading, and in fast peer-to-peer and cross-border payments. They indicate that in relation to the retail payments market the stablecoins operate as a "narrow bank". In this context stablecoins would be required to be backed by commercial bank reserves, themselves fully backed by central bank reserves. The authors suggest that the narrow bank approach is roughly equivalent to the form of retail CBDC adopted by China's e-CNY, in which the digital currency is a liability of the central bank but is accessed via a commercial bank or a fintech company like Alipay. The problem with this stablecoin model is that, according to the authors, it is likely to lead to significant disintermediation of the commercial bank deposits as customers use stablecoins for transaction purposes. However, it is not entirely clear why this would occur (see Chapter 4) and may be linked to the narrow bank definitions and usage in the US. An additional problem, as the authors suggest, would be a significantly increased demand for central bank reserves from stablecoin issuers, although this impact is not quantified.

Liao and Caramichael suggest an alternative, and preferred, structure for the use of stablecoins. In this model the stablecoins are backed by only a proportion of commercial bank deposits used for fractional reserve banking, ultimately being backed by a mixture of loans, assets and central bank reserves. The authors argue that this model for stablecoin accounts (or tokens) being held by commercial banks would be neutral as far as disintermediation is concerned as the stablecoin deposits would be treated in the same way as retail deposits. The authors do not deal with the issue raised above, in relation to Waller's comments, concerning the tendency to monopoly, given the potential for a major stablecoin company to become a dominant market player.

Implications of retail CBDCs for citizens

Insofar as a retail CBDC innovation is likely to alter, at least to some degree, the relationship between the citizen, commercial banks and the central bank, especially as it may also be accompanied by the introduction of some variety of distributed ledger technology (though not necessarily visible to the customers or merchants), then such an introduction will require careful management. This will entail – and the overall thinking of central banks appears to confirm this position, as will be shown – a likely gradualist approach and one which, at least initially, does not represent a major dislocation of existing monetary practice as far as the general public is concerned. The legal implications also require examination.

When a customer banks over the internet, they will not see the digital money, but only the adjusted balances, which represents the digital money holding of the account holder. Were a CBDC to be introduced in token form then the arbitrary lump sum involved would appear in an electronic wallet, held either directly by the customer or by their bank as custodian. Unlike the account balances the value of each token would never change, in the same way as cutting off a corner of a banknote does not alter its value. These crucial differences, but also similarities, between a digital currency and cash will be explained below, in relation to the various CBDC model design options.

DOMESTIC MONETARY AND LEGAL IMPLICATIONS

Before discussing the various design options and their differing implications, it will be useful to set out three *minimum* conditions that any modification to the current monetary system architecture, involving a retail CBDC, will have to meet, in order to provide the necessary functions and level of service to business and the general public.

Since the start of the industrial revolution a crucial issue has been the necessity of providing financial capital for a long-enough period to enable innovation to take place and the production of goods to be successfully delivered (Lloyd 2021). This involves the maturity transformation of short-term cash deposits into longer-term loans, although in modern monetary economies the actual process is reversed. First, contemporary monetary architecture achieves this maturity transformation indirectly, via cooperation between commercial banks and the central bank. The commercial bank creates a loan for a viable project for a creditworthy customer, together with a matching deposit (private money). This asset (loan) is eventually converted into a liability on the account of the central bank as a "reserve" (public money). At some point, the loan will be repaid, and the commercial bank asset, commercial bank deposit liability, and the central bank liability will all be extinguished. The introduction of a CBDC should not be allowed to interfere with this process. Second, to ensure the on-going ability of commercial banks to initiate and continue the above transformation it is imperative that the central bank provides a continuous supply of liquidity to permit the banks to do so. Failure to do so will lead to a financial crisis. Third, the central bank is also responsible, jointly with financial regulators (of which it is generally one), for maintaining the overall financial stability of the monetary system by ensuring the acceptability and credibility of both the financial institutions and the credit instruments. This function involves the final settlement provision to ensure that there is account balance for the monetary system, whatever the credit/debit balance of individual commercial banks.

Financial stability also involves ensuring that the introduction of retail CBDCs does not lead to sudden deposit withdrawals leading to bank runs (a potential problem already raised by several commentators in relation to any introduction of CBDCs). How real the problem is will depend very much on the modalities of the retail CBDC and how it is introduced.

These three key requirements must be preserved in the case of any modification of the monetary system. However, there may be other requirements, especially for businesses, to be met in the future, related to permitting the operation of innovative financial instruments, such as programmable "smart contracts"[3] (see Chapter 3).

---

3. "Smart contracts are simply programs stored on a blockchain that run when predetermined conditions are met. They typically are used to automate the execution of an agreement so that all participants can be immediately certain of the outcome,

Design options for CBDCs

There are a variety of design considerations that impact CBDCs ability to serve as a means of payment and a store of value. These include:

- *Anonymity/Privacy*. Society will have to decide on how far the need to protect an individual's privacy outweighs the need to prevent criminal behaviour and money laundering.
- *Transfers*. CBDCs may be transferred directly, on a peer-to-peer basis, or via an intermediary, such as a central bank, with whom a CBDC account is held.
- *Interest*. Digital money tokens or accounts could be interest-bearing, either positive (to enhance its attractiveness as a store of value) or non-interest bearing, as with cash. Essentially this is a monetary policy question.
- *Limits*. Quantitative limits on the amounts held or on their use during periods could be used. Such limits could be used to render CBDCs less attractive for wholesale payments.

The introduction of any of these features will have technological implications.

There are four main distinct models for a *retail* CBDC (Auer & Bohme 2021): direct, hybrid, intermediated and indirect.

Direct CBDC

Design for the first model will involve the central bank directly operating the payment system, by offering retail services directly to consumers and maintaining the ledger of all such transactions, with the CBDC involving *a direct claim on the central bank*. In this system the digital token is equivalent to a banknote.

The direct CBDC is attractive for its simplicity, as it eliminates dependence on intermediaries by doing away with them for retail CBDC operations. However, this choice would entail a substantial addition to central bank operations. Indeed, one of the reasons why this model is unpopular with central banks is because of the potential high level of technology required to provide a retail banking service to customers. The service would require a massive expansion of central bank operations, including responsibility for KYC compliance and due diligence, in the same way that commercial banks operate. It would require legislation in many countries to enable central banks to go well beyond their current mandates.

---

without any intermediary's involvement or time loss. They can also automate a workflow, triggering the next action when conditions are met" (IBM 2021a).

It would, of course, be possible – and probably necessary – for the central bank to contract out the operation of the retail banking service to either the private sector or another public sector organization. Such a move would entail extra costs and risks and as these would be taken on by the outsourced company, would entail extra costs to the retail consumer. The various costs and risks entailed in selecting this direct option – including having to deal with problems of off-line payments and potential connectivity outages – is a strong disincentive to using this model. Moreover, there is no guarantee of providing customers with an equivalent service to current bank retail transactions.

Hybrid/account-based or hybrid/token-based

In a hybrid CBDC, the model splits the payment system: the commercial banks (or other financial intermediaries) manage the retail transactions, and the central bank keeps a ledger recording the retail transactions, with a direct claim by the customer on the central bank.

Under this model it is possible to operate either as a token-based or as an account-based scheme. In both cases a key underpinning element of the hybrid CBDC model is the legal framework that segregates the claims on the CBDC from the balance sheets of the commercial banks/financial intermediaries. This segregation permits the separate CBDC holding and management to be transferred to another financial intermediary, in the event of the failure of an intermediary, protecting it from the creditors of the failed company. Technologically this is possible as the central bank has retained on its ledger a copy of the CBDC retail holdings and retail transactions.

As with the direct CBDC model, in the hybrid model there is security and resilience for the CBDC customer/client, provided by the role of the central bank, and the hybrid model is also simpler to operate for the central bank, as the management of the retail transactions of the account is handled by the financial intermediary. Nonetheless, the central bank is still faced with establishing a complex technological operating infrastructure.

Intermediated account-based

Again, private-sector financial intermediaries, principally commercial banks, manage the retail transactions in this model. However, they also maintain the ledger containing a record of all retail transactions. The central bank maintains a central ledger of only the corresponding wholesale transactions, matching the retail activity. Again, there remains a direct CBDC user claim on the central bank.

One of the problems raised by CBDCs concerns the potential impact on disintermediation, in which commercial banks *may* lose their private money deposits to CBDCs (see EY 2021 and ECB 2020b). Awareness of the problem has led to consideration of both the intermediated account-based model and a final indirect intermediated model considered below.

Aside from the fact that the CBDC consumer/client retains a direct claim on the central bank, this model operates in the same way as the familiar two-tier, wholesale CBDC system, with the account-holding commercial bank/financial intermediary holding the KYC authentication and executing all retail payments and account management, including maintenance of a retail transactions ledger. The role of the central bank in this model is simply to maintain a wholesale payments "mirror" ledger record, corresponding to the retail balances kept by the commercial bank/financial intermediary, thus ensuring final settlement, as is done in the prevailing monetary architecture.

What is currently unclear is the legal position in the event of a dispute, and whether the CBDC holder would take legal action against the central bank alone or both the central bank and the commercial bank. Presumably the central bank may also wish to act against the commercial bank. There may need to be government legislation to clarify the position and avoid unnecessary litigation.

Indirect account-based

In this model variant, there is no direct CBDC claim on the central bank, instead any claim on the central bank is held by the intermediaries, which also manage and record all the retail transactions (Vox.EU 2021). It could be argued that, as this variant does not permit any direct customer claim on the central bank, it should not be regarded as a CBDC, but as a digital currency is still issued, this seems untenable (see below). All retail transaction management, recording and claims are the responsibility of the financial intermediaries. However, these intermediary liabilities to their retail customers, as with current practice, are backed with claims on the central bank.

This model is sometimes referred to in the literature as the "two-tier" CBDC, for its close resemblance to the prevailing two-tier financial system operated by commercial banks and the central bank. Moreover, in this model the commercial bank must fully back each outstanding indirect CBDC-like liability to the consumer/client.

As in today's banking system, the commercial bank/financial intermediary handles all communication with retail clients. In settlement activity the commercial bank/financial intermediary nets payments, sends payment messages to other intermediaries, and wholesale payment instructions to the central bank. The latter then finally settles wholesale CBDC balances/accounts.

In this indirect model, the bank operation is solely concerned with receiving the CBDC digital money deposit from the central bank and then handling any transactions involving the digital money deposited (Auer & Böhme 2020). The commercial bank will thus handle all communication with the retail client, will net payments made and send accompanying payment messages to other financial intermediaries, then send wholesale payment instructions to the central bank. The central bank then settles wholesale accounts with finality. It is expected that this model would utilize an account balance structure, although it would also work with a token-based system (Ali 2018).

Notwithstanding the above brief description of the apparent similarity of this design with today's familiar banking system, there will be a need to establish regulatory and supervisory control, especially in terms of protecting client digital money deposits. This would certainly be the case if a financial intermediary/internet payments provider decided to establish a "narrow banking"[4] operation based on the indirect model.

Consumer access to the CBDC

Customer access to account-based CBDC and indirect models is relatively simple and potentially similar to customers currently accessing their current/checking accounts and deposit accounts, via a personal or corporate identity scheme. However, it remains to be seen how popular CBDC-issued digital money will be with potential customers. To an extent the popularity will depend on the choice of model variant and on the security offered to the customer, together with convenience and efficiency, and off-line connectivity.

The issue is not yet resolved and is clearly relevant to the choice between direct token-based access (such as adopted by the Bahamas), hybrid (token-based or account-based), intermediated models, and indirect access models. Although not a large group in developed countries, as they are in developing or emerging market countries, the issue of access for those who are unbanked and/or rely on cash for many payments is still significant, and requires attention. For instance, in the UK a recent survey published in March 2022 (Hall *et al.* 2022) suggested that 10 million UK citizens, one in five, rely on cash. Irrespective of the use of token-based CBDC approaches, the issues of access to cash in many countries raises issues of strong public concern. In European countries other than the UK this concern is evident. The following extract from a BIS paper on the CBDC position in the Czech Republic demonstrates the point.

---

4. Narrow banking essentially entails loans are only issued against secured deposits.

As far as this relates to the Czech Republic, it can be said that the trend of decreasing cash usage in some countries is going in the opposite direction in the Czech Republic (where cash in circulation is still rising both in absolute terms and relative to GDP), despite the Covid-19 pandemic crisis. Trends in currency in circulation in the Czech Republic are comparable to those in the euro area, Poland, the United Kingdom and United States. The problem of public access to cash is therefore not relevant in the Czech Republic, even after the first waves of the pandemic. Although it seems that the ratio of electronic to cash payments has increased, this has not affected the volume of cash in circulation.

(Vodrážka *et al.* 2021: 66)

Currently, nine central banks have indicated that they are leaning towards indirect (tiered) access; seven towards intermediated account-based access, and five, including the Bahamas, considering, or even implementing, direct token-based access (Auer, Cornelli & Frost 2021). This last group are mostly developing countries, especially multi-island nations.

A token-based system would ensure universal access – as anybody can obtain a digital signature – and it would offer privacy by default, assuming users keep their key secure. It would also allow the CBDC to interface with communication protocols that are likely to be the basis for micropayments within the "internet of things". This is known as a programmable, "smart contract" payment system where the payments are automatically transferred, without any prior authorization (see below). However, the privacy (suggested as a benefit) would, unless constrained in some way, also permit evasion of AML/CFT rules. The design of a CBDC has also to cover transactional privacy. The personal financial date involved in a transaction between two parties may be able to reveal the personal information to a third party.

Consumers' need for cash-like payment safety from a digital money token or from a digital money account, requires a CBDC to be secure from technology failures of the financial intermediaries and of power outages or "denial of service" hacking at the central bank, as well as from cash-flow problems at any financial intermediary. How far this may be guaranteed will be part of the design specification, noting that the *complete* anonymity provided by cash will not be possible with its digital equivalent, nor is it possible to provide a 100 per cent guarantee of technological failure or from hacking. These issues also involve how, and in what form, distributed ledger and blockchain technology, and the accruing benefits from their use, can be incorporated into the technology used to implement CBDCs (see Chapter 3).

Some 27 banks are currently actively considering one or other of the last three retail CBDC models outlined above. While the direct model design is not favoured, discussion of the various CBDC model designs has indicated both positive and negative features of each. Some central banks favour hybrid-based approaches and some others the use of decentralized database platforms (see Chapter 3 for discussion on technology choices), although all are generally conservative in their approach.

The position that appears likely to be adopted by the majority of central banks is the one that most closely resembles the current-day monetary system. Central banks are cautious by nature and will not want to radically disturb the existing monetary system. Perhaps the US, with its desire to protect competition, may seek to establish a monetary structure that supports both public money (CBDCs) and private money (stablecoins). Banking operations that are currently experienced by the general public are likely to continue to be maintained, implemented via either the retail CBDC indirect model or the hybrid intermediated, account-based model.

It remains to be seen whether pressure from the private sector development of stablecoin operational design and usage, especially by large corporate groups and the financial sector, will continue to exert pressure on central banks, causing them to bring forward the prospective piloting and introduction of CBDCs. The testing of "use cases" on the general public by central banks may also shed some light on the retail CBDC choices to be made, during a decade when digitization of daily lives will continue to increase, and the use of cash for payments will continue to decline. However, the problem with use-cases is that without some clear definition of the operation of the CBDC design model to be launched, offered to both business-users and to the public, they are of little more value than opinion surveys.

The decline of cash, although not taken to the point where it disappears, is likely to continue over time, together with the continuing private sector digital innovation in finance, which will lead almost inevitably to consideration of CBDCs by all central banks. The choice of the most appropriate model should entail a continuing dialogue between consumers/clients, commercial banks and payment service providers, and central banks, to ensure that bank customers' needs and business operations are fully catered for in response to technological innovation. Chapter 6 examines how the widest possible consultation on the issue, prior to any implementation, might be handled.

Legal implications

In consideration of CBDCs much of the attention has been focused on the conceptual and technological design and facilitation of central bank issuance of digital money directly to the business and the general public. Less attention has been paid to the legal framework within which money/credit, public and private, is set. The nature and role of money, and of the central bank, working in concert with commercial banks, has been described in the context of political economy. The impact of CBDCs, and the varying impact of them on consumers, dependent on the design chosen, has also been discussed. Chapter 4 will discuss the impacts on the commercial banking sector. It is also important to examine the various legal issues arising from the introduction of CBDCs. In what follows on the key legal issues, I am indebted to the contributions of a number of authors and especially Zellweger-Gutknecht (2021) and Bossu *et al.* (2020).

Both authors agree that new legislation will be required as the result of any final proposal to introduce CBDCs. Indeed, the IMF Working Paper (Bossu) offers a proposed draft of such legislation. They only differ (although it is an important difference) in respect of whether or not the introduction of CBDCs issued in the form of account balances differs from issuance as tokens. Zellweger-Gutknecht suggests that there is no difference. The IMF paper argues that only if issues are as tokens is digital money equivalent to cash. Throughout this book, the view of Zellweger-Gutknecht is the one taken, notwithstanding the need to be aware of the different treatment insofar as digital money balances are "malleable" in terms of the value of credits and debits, whereas when digital money is represented by tokens, its value is fixed.

The position of Zellweger-Gutknecht is explained in the following paragraph:

> In summary, account balances are money, but tokens are no less so. Both are transferred by debit and credit, since tokens are also invalidated or rather fully debited and newly created or credited with each transaction. The authors of current monetary laws simply had not encountered digital tokens when they drafted the legislation. Therefore, if a provision mentions 'accounts', this is not legally a qualified silence in the sense that all other digital forms of representation would be inadmissible. A policy paper recently published by IMF authors reached a different conclusion (Bossu *et al.* 2020). However, it seems to be based on a rather formalistic and literal interpretation of the relevant laws. A conclusive assessment by academic papers would only be possible, however, if the authors were to publish the raw data used in their analysis, which would be extremely important in view of the issue's topicality and the weight attached to IMF assessments in general.
>
> (Zellweger-Gutknecht 2021: 34)

More simply, Zellweger-Gutknecht, correctly in my view, is suggesting that in opposition to the IMF position, that whether the CBDC is issued as tokens or is issued in the form of account balances it is *still* digital money. The IMF seem to be confused by the use of the term "digital currency", where "currency" is defined as an official means of payment, and the more appropriate designation in economic terms as "digital money" (see UK Parliament House of Lords Economic Committee exchange on a question asked by Lord King (Cunliffe 2021b)).

Zellweger-Gutknecht further argues that:

> Consequently, an architecture that avoids direct interaction between the public and the central bank and, in particular, does not create a contractual relationship between them but continues to regulate their relationship solely by public law should be chosen. The issuance and transfer of digital cash will be handled by financial intermediaries on behalf of and for the account of the central bank. As a result, both tokens and account balances will continue to be recorded on the liabilities side of the central bank. This architecture would safeguard the essential risk-free nature of cash and prevent the state from easily obtaining insight into the public's financial transactions, while simultaneously preserving the banks' information about their customers' payment flows, which remain essential for risk-adequate lending.
>
> (Zellweger-Gutknecht 2021: 35)

This approach would probably rule out use of the direct tokenized CBDC model option. In practice, as already intimated, the preferred approach of most central banks may, in any event, favour an account-based indirect or intermediated CBDC model. Although it would still leave the design option of the hybrid model, currently favoured by China.

This legal approach would essentially leave in place the current wholesale digital monetary system, in which competition between commercial banks generally determines the supply of money in the economy, although adjustment of the legal rules, such as those covering central banks, would still be required. Insofar as a more adventurous approach were to be taken to the introduction of retail CBDCs, such as a hybrid token-based system, then there would have to be substantial legal changes to the current framework within which central banks are governed.

In summary, there are essentially three main areas of legal concern. First, there is how the impact of CBDCs will affect the general position of central banks in relation to the legal remit and governance structures under which they operate (as indicated above). Second, there are the legal implications of the monetary and operational impacts on commercial banks of the introduction of CBDCs (see Chapter 4). Third, there are the legal implications of any subsequent move, following the introduction of CBDCs, to use the CBDC allocations to individual citizens to directly target them in pursuance of monetary policy objectives (discussed in the next section of this chapter). There is also the unresolved question of whether CBDCs would have the status of legal tender, although it seems likely that they would. This issue has been raised in the context of the Swedish retail CBDC project, and also by the IMF (Ledger Insights 2020).

The legal situation in the UK, for instance, relating to the powers and operations of the Bank of England, is governed by the various Banking Acts, originating in modern times with the 1946 Act and supplemented by successive further Acts, especially the 1998 Act. The introduction of digital money via a retail CBDC, whichever model option is selected, would have significant social, economic and political implications, directly affecting the current legal and regulatory framework surrounding and governing the actions of the Bank of England, and are likely to entail some amendments to this UK legislation. The need for, and amount of, legal changes will vary across monetary jurisdictions. For instance, in the eurozone where the distribution of monetary functions is complex and in the US, as a federal country, the legal ramifications may be complicated.

As far as the legal requirements relating to commercial banks are concerned, the primary concern is the potential for disintermediation. The issue itself will be examined in the next chapter, but it is worth anticipating here some legal changes that may be required. The ECB would appear to be likely to have constitutional legal issues (Nabilou 2019) to contend with in introducing a CBDC, and it is useful to use the EU as an example here. If the disintermediation were to, as it almost certainly would, interfere with the "smooth conduct of policies pursued by the competent authorities relating to the prudential supervision of credit institutions and the stability of the financial system" (see Article 127(6) of the TFEU), then this would damage the statutory mandate to pursue the policies. A further potential legal problem of a CBDC covering the eurozone – although not necessarily confined to the eurozone – is that CBDCs could lead to a centralization of credit allocation, rather than, as at present, being generally the province of decentralized commercial banks. In the case of the ECB, it is constitutionally obliged to act so as *not to undermine* "the principle of an open market economy with free competition" (Article 127 of the TFEU and Article 2 of Protocol 4 of the Statute of the European System of Central Banks and the ECB). Another potential legal problem for CBDCs relates to the role of cash in relation to payment systems within financial market infrastructures (FMIs) that are governed by international rules set by CPMI and IOSCO, and which give legal and natural persons access to FMIs.

The suggestion that monetary policy may be targeted directly at individuals to control consumer spending (see next section), would certainly give rise to a number of legitimate legal concerns about the permissible extent of monetary policy operated by central banks.

The IMF paper (Bossu *et al.* 2020) raises some similar legal issues to those dealt with above, although suggesting, correctly, that, to an extent the legal status of CBDCs partly depends on the operational and technical design features. The degree of new legislative action will vary across jurisdictions, as the remits of some central banks may well already permit CBDC issuance. In some jurisdictions central banks are legally empowered to open accounts for the general public, in others this may have to be granted.

The IMF argues that, conceptually, monetary law is about the powers of the state to issue a currency and is typically outlined in a constitution. Hence, it may be the case that to even consider token-based CBDCs to be legally equivalent to banknotes requires significant reform. The IMF questions whether a CBDC should have blanket "legal tender" status – where people or organizations have to accept the currency as payment – given that parts of the population may not technically be capable of using it. It was suggested that legal tender status be limited to "sophisticated entities" such as the state itself, public bodies, large firms and financial institutions.

The IMF paper concludes that: "Overall, before CBDCs are issued, they need a 'robust, ideally explicit, legal basis', and only a few central banks offer this. Central bank laws can be easily changed, but monetary ones not so much. Countries will need to carefully consider the potential amendments of existing laws or the creation of laws before CBDC issuance" (Bossu 2020: 41)

Although in some jurisdictions there may well be constitutional issues which need to be resolved – and although in many countries there may have to be legislative amendment and reform to protect institutions and organizations, public and private – it seems unlikely that there will be insurmountable legal barriers to introducing CBDCs. However, in some jurisdictions, including the EU, there may be political hurdles to be overcome, as well as legal ones.

Monetary policy implications

Conventional monetary policy implementation involves the central bank using their balance sheets to control short-term interest rates. This is done via open market operations (buying and selling government securities) to provide or absorb liquidity, and thus maintain the desired level of central bank reserves. CBDCs would simply *add* to the current demands for reserves from commercial banks. This may well, dependent on the size of the extra demand for reserves, lead to an increase in the size of the central bank balance sheet required to maintain interest rates at the desired level. CBDC demand may, of course, also prove to be more volatile, rendering monetary policy more difficult to manage. Were CBDCs to be interest-bearing then this would be an added complication, but not altering the above overall picture.

Notwithstanding the general point made above – that the issue of accommodating CBDCs for monetary policy purposes is a quantitative rather than a qualitative impact – the increased, and possibly extended range of assets used to meet the CBDC demand may well need to be reviewed. Their varying maturity, liquidity, and credit risk characteristics may be difficult to predict, especially across different jurisdictions. Monetary policies have become increasingly complex over the past two decades, with a substantial reliance placed on monetary policy vis-à-vis fiscal policy in managing aggregate demand. A further innovation, such as that represented by the advent of retail CBDCs, will require detailed examination in relation to the future operation of monetary policy

There have been some suggestions, from academics and, informally, from some central banks (Panetta 2021) that the conventional policy could be supplemented by a non-conventional (and controversial) approach. It would be *possible* to use a CBDC – providing the digital money *directly* to citizens – to influence consumer spending directly, either via imposing negative interest rates on the issues of CBDCs or by time-limiting the spending of CBDC money. The discussion on these suggestions is in its infancy and is contentious. Various central banks and banking think tanks, such as the US Bank Policy Institute, and other economic experts, are distinctly unenthusiastic about the idea.

There is an argument that monetary policy would be enhanced by the creation of a CBDC. For instance, currently the velocity of money (V) is a theoretical concept. Economists try to calculate it, but the calculation is ambiguous because they are not able to quantify "V". A CBDC could be used to determine its magnitude as a monetary variable, directly identifying consumer expenditure on goods and services. "V" – assuming that a CBDC design provided digital money directly to citizens – *could* be targeted and enable the central bank to directly influence consumer spending, via the digital money holdings of the general public. However, there are significant reasons for being concerned about this potential development – some have argued that it would lead to government surveillance and the ability, for instance, to introduce a "social credit" scheme.

In relation to monetary policy, a comparison could be drawn between the current preferred central banks' monetary policy of asset purchase programmes – supplemented by forward guidance (and, in the case of the ECB and Japan, of negative interest rates) – and the advent of retail CBDCs which would *potentially* offer a more targeted approach to individual consumer demand management. However, such an approach would be more akin to the use of a fiscal policy instrument than to monetary policy action

One issue, in terms of retail CBDC model design selection, is whether use of the indirect model would possibly inhibit use of such a policy. The structure and operation in this model is so close to being a replication of the contemporary central bank–commercial bank model that operating such an innovative monetary policy would be difficult to conceive. Any suggestion of modifying monetary policy in this manner is likely to be contentious (Zellweger-Gutknecht 2021) and will require more substantial discussion than is possible here, including wide public discussion. However, the substantive issues forming the debate can be outlined.

Zellweger-Gutknecht argues that according to current legal practice in most countries, neither direct restriction nor expansion of cash is an instrument of monetary policy. Hence, should such a policy be introduced – for instance by positive or negative interest rates on CBDCs – then this policy would require a change in the law. She further argues, trenchantly, that such a move would "violate the price stability mandate and the principle of an open market economy" (Zellweger-Gutknecht 2021: 36).

It is not clear that the use of such a new monetary policy instrument would, necessarily, damage a price stability objective or that it would jeopardize the principle of an open economy. Rather, the objections would more likely be that it was an obtrusive intervention in people's personal freedom to spend, with potentially damaging social and economic welfare repercussions.

Any such move to a direct monetary policy intervention, by a central bank, to influence the ability of individuals to spend would also raise questions about the apparently well-established convention of having, in Western countries, independent, technocratic central banks. Were such a monetary instrument be proposed, it would be argued that any such policy would need to be democratically approved, thus restoring either government or parliamentary control over the central bank.

Patently, the projected use of cash/digital money as a direct monetary policy instrument does raise, as suggested, social, economic and political questions, as well as the need to adjust the current legal constraints. Nonetheless, if monitoring and even controlling the use of digital cash proves, on examination, to be a more efficient *and* a more *equitable* monetary policy measure, then its use should surely be considered, and a judgement made of the implications, for and against.

For instance, as discussed in Bojkova *et al.* (2020), the favoured and extensive utilization of sovereign bond purchases by central banks, is inequitable, as it has increased relative wealth inequalities via increased asset prices, principally held by the rich. Moreover, it is not clear, despite claims by central banks, that the various policies, including asset purchases, operated by central banks in attempts to stimulate economic growth have achieved this aim in an equitable manner.

The two key issues, which monetary policy attempts indirectly and directly to address, required for stimulating economic growth, are increased productivity and increased aggregate consumer demand. The advent of CBDCs, directly impacting on the equivalent of cash, would provide an ability to directly increase the velocity of circulation of money, and hence consumer spending, and thereby indirectly stimulating business capital investment and productivity. In this context there would be little distinction between monetary policy and *fiscal* policy.[5]

The balance of arguments in this area of policy are nuanced, as is suggested. Monetary policy cost-benefit analyses related to CBDC should be conducted and may need to be revisited periodically. If the cost-benefit analyses of all the factors involved – including the ones raised by Zellweger-Gutknecht, and ones relating to personal freedoms – indicate a significant positive net benefit, then it *might* then be appropriate for any requisite legal changes to be authorized. In any event any decision will need to be carefully balanced.

Cross-border payments

The above sections have covered the interest of central banks in their exploration of domestic retail CBDCs and crucially the economic, monetary and legal implications of such an innovation. We can now turn to the use of an extended wholesale CBDC for cross-border payments, which is receiving extremely close attention by central banks across the world.

As outlined earlier, central banks are already making pre-emptive moves, under the aegis of the BIS, to *prototype* a wholesale CBDC (wCBDC) methodology, *potentially* extending RTGS systems in multicurrency cross-border payment environments for substantial bank-funded transfers, and providing for other corporate retail assets transfer, such as corporate securities. Other cross-border projects, independent of the BIS, are also being pursued.

Notwithstanding, the above development, which will cater for the major financial transfers relating to trade and capital investment, there will likely be demands for lower value cross-border transfers, often relating to tourism or to remittances from people working away from their homeland and sending money back to their families. As indicated in Chapter 1, with reference to the Nigerian Naira retail CBDC, the demand for such a transfer of funds across borders, from citizens of the country concerned, can be accommodated in this manner via a retail CBDC, with appropriate safeguards.

It would, of course, be possible for the need for low-value transfers to be accommodated within a wholesale cross-border CBDC system. However, as will

---

5. Monetary policy involves central bank action on monetary instruments, including interest rates, bond purchases, monetary aggregates and credit controls. Fiscal policy involves national government action on consumer and business spending via adjustment of tax rates and grants.

be discussed in Chapter 3, there will be technological limits on a retail CBDC system requiring a large number of correspondents/participants/nodes to be held on the system, because of scalability limits.

For the task of managing low-cost and rapid financial transfers the current global financial system is complex, risky, slow and expensive, although over recent years there has been a decline in the numbers of correspondent banks involved in the transactions. The advent of novel digital technology, being exploited by the private sector and corporations, offers not only a challenge to central banks. For instance, stablecoins are using blockchain and DLT for intra-company transfers across borders (see Liao & Caramichael 2022). However, the technology also offers an opportunity for central banks to use it for central bank fiat currency cross-border transfers. The route that some central banks are now exploring is to utilize wholesale CBDC (wCBDC) to support a safe, fiat currency *tokenized* cross-border, ecosystem. The projects (outlined in the Appendices) are based on semi-decentralized distributed ledger technology, including blockchain, and are exploring use-cases that provide access to central bank money for regulated financial institutions engaged in significant level cross-border financial transfers. The underlying technology issues involved are discussed in Chapter 3.

There is also concern that, if central banks are left behind in providing appropriate cross-border architectures, then future DLT private money transfer platforms could emerge, involving multiple assets and currencies, for instance using Ripple's Interledger platform (Ripple 2021). There are, of course, already private money transfer channels, but currently they use a structure of correspondent commercial banks. However, unless coordinated, central banks could also employ different DLT platforms, set up by different central banks for cross-border transfers, potentially leading to global liquidity problems. Hence, the BIS is involved in several projects to develop a *prototype* system that would also lead to an international standard of interoperability between wCBDC settlement platforms. Technical feasibility may be less of a problem, save for some constraints on scalability and on interoperability, than the ability of central banks globally to agree on the policy choices they have now to face.

Drawing up a balance sheet, even in purely qualitative terms, is problematic because of the variability of the CBDC model designs which could be used and the costs and benefits of each of the models. Moreover, at present, there is no clear consensus. This is one reason why the qualitative terms – advantages and disadvantages – are used rather than quantifiable costs and benefits. Table 2.1 is simply an attempt to point up some of the key points raised by the various protagonists in the debate. The assumption is made that the intermediated retail CBDC model design is the one selected for the comparison, although the further assumption is made that an API layer will separate the central bank ledger,

Table 2.1 The pros and cons of CBDCs

Advantages	Disadvantages
Retail CBDCs	
Greater efficiency of transactions, in terms of speed and lower cost	Potential disintermediation
Enhanced prevention of illicit activities	Concerns about increased state control
Financial inclusion via smartphones and off-line payment cards	Potentially less private sector innovation
Potentially more effective monetary policy instruments	Problems with interoperability: digital access
Wholesale CBDCs	
Lower costs for international payments	Potential for reduced competition
Competition for high-cost private transfers	Increased influence of central banks
Enhancement of global financial stability	

probably some variant of DLT, and the public interface. *If* retail CBDCs are introduced, especially in developed modern economies, then this seems likely to be the most favoured route. Wholesale CBDCs for cross-border financial transfers are far more likely to be introduced.

Conclusion

The importance of central bank money (fiat) money is difficult to overstate. It provides the central trust anchor for today's monetary system and underpins the trust that citizens have in their currencies. Whatever the enhanced, technology-driven role of private money channels, beyond the role of commercial banks, the role of public money – fiat currencies issued by central banks – will still be required. Unless tightly regulated, stablecoins provide a potential threat to the fundamental role of central banks and the trust-anchor position of their issue of fiat currency in the monetary system. It is worth noting that the US position on CBDCs is currently unclear, with apparent reluctance to endorse the establishment of a US CBDC being evinced by commercial banks (US Bank Policy Institute 2021), and by some members of the Federal Reserve Board (Waller 2021), despite the more positive position of the US administration.

The *minimum* conditions that any modification to the current monetary system architecture, involving a CBDC, will have to meet are to maintain adequate maturity transformation; to sustain intermediation; to ensure sufficient liquidity provision to meet increased demand for reserves; and to avoid any weakening of the financial stability of the monetary system.

The only hard evidence to date as to which of the four[6] potential CBDC models will be selected by central banks is of the choices made by China (hybrid model), The Bahamas (direct, token-based) and Nigeria (direct account-based). However, especially given the strong advice being given by the BIS and the desire of most central banks to avoid significant disruption to their existing monetary systems, it seems likely that either indirect or intermediate account-based systems for *retail* CBDCs may be the choice of the majority of central banks in developed jurisdictions. Although even in these jurisdictions, the issue of the access for unbanked or cash-preference customers, would be a problem to be addressed.

Conventional monetary policy is unlikely to be substantially altered by the introduction of CBDCs, of themselves, although in quantitative terms the central bank role of supplying reserves to meet the extra demand – in order to maintain the target real short-term interest rate – may require some adjustments, such as provision of different but acceptable collateral.

Potentially, although controversially, there could be innovative use of retail CBDCs in relation to the use of more direct consumer management of spending via monetary policy. This debate has barely begun, and certainly not yet in the public square. There is likely to be considerable resistance to any such moves, from groups representing consumers and more widely, including from some governments, certainly in the short to medium term. The introduction of such measures would also, because of a blurring of the distinction between monetary policy and fiscal policy, throw into question the issue of central bank independence from governments. Hence, the potential for introducing a new monetary policy instrument by directly varying the digital money made available to citizens/consumers as a means of controlling consumer demand will raise a variety of social, economic, political and legal issues. All of these would require careful consideration before any such innovation was considered.

The legal position in relation to the governance of central banks will need to be reviewed if retail CBDCs are introduced, although any changes required will vary as between jurisdictions. If the suggested supplementation of conventional monetary policy was considered more wide-ranging, as indicated above, legal changes would be more extensive, including perhaps reviewing the political independence of central banks.

---

6.   It is worth indicating that the (IMF 2022) provides a three-fold nomenclature of CBDC models, unilateral, intermediated and synthetic. This classification overlaps the BIS classification, which is used in this book.

There is growing evidence from the number and nature of projects being undertaken, that, in relation to cross-border payments – especially the potential for globally destabilizing private transfers – the position of central banks, led by the BIS, is to favour the establishment of regional, multicurrency *wholesale* CBDC structures, to facilitate these financial transfers. Lower-value cross-border transfers involving *retail* CBDC transfers may also be accommodated, although there will be some constraints. In utilizing DLT technology, remittances, as the Nigerian retail CBDC system shows, may be dealt with in another manner. A complementary role of private sector transfers, including the use of stablecoins together with central banks and commercial banks, has yet to be considered, but may be able to be accommodated.

3
TECHNOLOGY

The database technologies available for CBDCs are either centralized, decentralized, or semi-decentralized databases. The use of distributed ledger technology (DLT), or a "bespoke" version of blockchain, which maintains a measure of centralized control by the central bank, are the main options for both retail and wholesale CBDCs. The issue for central banks will be whether the financial data of a distributed group of participants can be collectively and safely maintained, without internal system reliance on a single central party or a centralized data store. Whatever variant of CBDC is selected, it must offer scalability, confidentiality/privacy, availability/latency and security/resilience.

There are four technology decisions, all relating to the potential design model choices to be made by central banks for both retail CBDCs and wholesale CBDCs. First, the choice between a central ledger database technology (the current position) versus a decentralized, distributed database technology. Second, should a fully decentralized database technology prove too problematic for central banks, is a semi-decentralized approach practical and how exactly does this choice involve DLT/blockchain technology? Third, how do the database choices relate to the use-cases for wholesale CBDCs for cross-border applications and the available retail CBDC model design options? Finally, how best to establish interoperability between differing database approaches and maintain technological innovation over time.

Central vs decentralized databases

As far as retail CBDCs are concerned the decision has yet to be made, although it seems likely that DLT, in some format, will be used for establishing retail CBDCs, albeit often under an API. Scalability is a key issue for retail CBDCs, whereas wholesale CBDCs when used for cross-border transfers involve a smaller number of participants on the network.

Traditionally, central bank databases have been centralized. Network centralization developed, historically, as a means to improve efficiency and take advantage of potential economies of scale. On the other hand, decentralization seeks to improve the speed and flexibility of networks by decentralizing computer processing across the network to the individual user (Brookings 2020).

Centralized ledgers, as used by central banks in the current monetary system architecture, provide a complete overview of wholesale transactions, demands for which they receive from commercial banks for clearance and settlement, using the movement of reserves to do so. Given the crucial role of central banks in maintaining trust in the monetary system, having centralized control of the ledger is a convenient and secure way of maintaining that trust-anchor role. An attendant danger that has to be constantly guarded against is the potential for the centralized nature of the database to be a vulnerable single point of failure, such as from a critical power outage or a malicious cyber-attack.

Hence, the advantages of centralized databases for central banks are primarily that they offer the overall control sought by central banks in their desire to provide a trusted anchor for the monetary system, based on their fiat currency. However, insofar as introducing a retail CBDC is concerned, if direct issuance to the general public were to be involved then the weak resilience of the centralized structure to the possibility of a catastrophic failure, such as the Equifax failure in 2017 (Equifax 2018), may rule out centralization. It should be noted however, that decentralized databases are not immune to failure, although the damage incurred may be less severe; for instance, a denial-of-service attack on the consensus mechanism. Various technological models are being explored, including using an API between a DLT/blockchain ledger and public access, such as that proposed by the Bank of England (Bank of England 2021c).

A decentralized ledger is a network of separate participants' ledgers that allow the central "controller" to combine the data in the separate ledgers into a complete record of all transactions and holdings. The periodicity could be daily or more frequently. Unfortunately, this structure would permit as many points of failure or error as nodes on the network, in addition to the central node. A middle way, to avoid the problems associated with both centralized and full decentralized database approaches, would entail a semi-decentralized structure, in which a consortium of entities collaboratively manages the system via a cryptographically enabled consensus mechanism. The consortium network is run over a distributed ledger, with a consensus relationship between the group of independent operators. The ledger and its data are available to all operators/users and remains so in the event of the failure of one or a limited number of the users' server nodes. A distributed ledger may be programmed to provide a complete record of all transactions across all participants in the distributed network, with identical copies distributed over all participants at all locations. A distributed ledger is also able to programme "smart contracts", which are stored on the ledger and automatically executed when predetermined terms and conditions are met. The synchronous updating of the shared ledger is achieved cryptographically, via a consensus algorithm that ensures secure and rapid updating across all locations on the network.

It should be noted that, despite its attraction for use with CBDCs, the semi-decentralized technological approach does not provide total digital money decentralized anonymity and the privacy of cash. On the other hand, the restrictions on the digital money involved do enable regulators and police to track money laundering and other financial crimes.

Notwithstanding its advantages, it is not yet possible to select a single omnibus version of a distributed ledger (or blockchain) suitable for all central banks to use for establishing CBDCs. Even where wholesale CBDCs are concerned, the distributed ledger will require tailoring to meet the requirements of the application concerned. For example, in cross-border applications of wholesale CBDCs, participants will be limited in number and the transaction messaging will be peer to peer across nodes, and not necessarily in blocks. These limitations are to take account of scalability and audit reporting requirements. For retail CBDC applications there are greater problems of scalability and privacy to be faced.

Distributed ledger technology

A distributed ledger generates a complete record of transactions and holdings across a network, with identical copies at all nodes on the network of participants avoiding the single point of failure danger of a centralized database. In a decentralized ledger there is still a central control system responsible for managing the individual separate nodal ledgers, or rather the data which is collected and combined from them. Whereas a distributed ledger may be cryptographically programmed to resolve potential conflicts when generating simultaneous updates, avoiding the necessity for continuous centralized control. It enables self-enforcing "smart contracts" to be executed across the ledger as a mechanism to update the ledger. A cryptographic solution, combined with a further consensus mechanism confirming agreement across all the network participants' nodes, provides the possibility of a shared ledger operating across all locations, with continuous updating of secure and transparent data.

From a CBDC perspective the DLT consensus mechanism (see the Inthanon project described in the Appendices) needs to provide finality in execution of transactions. After total finality (non-reversibility/immutability) has been reached across the validating nodes, committed transactions cannot be retroactively changed. However, such finality is problematic, except with a comparatively small set of validating nodes, because the higher the messaging overhead, the larger the set of nodes. For cross-border wholesale CBDCs, and for a central bank processing the wholesale data provided by trusted commercial banks, as in the contemporary monetary systems, this is not a problem. The network of nodes is relatively small, and scalability is not therefore an issue and finality is achievable.

DLT has several advantages, these include increased system reliability and resilience, integrity, transparency and security, although there may be a trade-off between performance and security (Kannengießer *et al.* 2020). One potential advantage of using DLT is the high level of operational resilience it offers by avoiding a single point of failure and maintained availability. Hence, DLT might offer a considerably increased level of resilience, potentially more efficiently and cheaply.

Privacy is one of the reasons why full decentralization, in the form of a not-be-spoke blockchain, is not being considered by the financial sector in connection with retail CBDCs. Instead, as indicated above, some form of *semi*-decentralization is advocated. The underlying financial database structures can be considered as a DLT or even as a bespoke blockchain. Effectively, these databases are tailored structures in response to the specific requirements of the CBDCs. The establishment and maintenance of trust is paramount and may initially be established by recruiting only trusted members (such as regulated commercial banks) to the "consortium". Trust is maintained through consensus mechanisms that limit privacy to only those party to the financial transaction, supported by cryptographic control mechanisms. The consortium blockchain in Project Jura is an example of this bespoke approach being used by central banks (sometimes a consortium blockchain is referred to as a "federated" blockchain).

There is a useful discussion of the issue from both a technical and policy viewpoint by Kannengießer:

> The specialization of ledgers regarding the policy archetype predominantly comes at the cost of opaqueness-related DLT characteristics (i.e., *traceability, transaction content visibility*, or *user unidentifiability*) and, additionally, *confidentiality* (due to transaction content visibility) and *throughput*. New regulations and standards are often introduced, and distributed ledgers must adapt to them to achieve compliance. Due to the high targeted level of integrity, the ex-post adaptation of a distributed ledger to reach compliance becomes challenging. For example, it is not possible to become compliant with the requirements imposed by the General Data Protection of the European Union (GDPR) when personal data are stored on a distributed ledger because GDPR demands for a possibility to completely delete personally-identifiable user

data. To increase flexibility to adapt applications on DLT to future regulations or standards, developers must carefully determine which data should be stored on-chain or off-chain. For now, it remains unclear how to provide flexibility to become compliant with future regulations or standards and achieve a high level of integrity at the same time. Therefore, sensitive data should be predominantly stored off-chain. Nevertheless, off-chain data stores are controlled by at least one trusted third party, which lowers the degree of decentralization of applications on DLT. In addition, external data need to be kept confidential and available for the distributed ledger. Thus, reliable interoperability of DLT designs with oracles[1] becomes important for the policy archetype. Furthermore, the oracles themselves must also be compliant with the same laws and regulations. (Kannengießer *et al.* 2020: 26–7).

The aim should be to insert updates into ledgers so that they apply protocol changes to comply with regulations and ISO standards.

Conventional centralized and DLT-based infrastructures both store data multiple times and in physically separate locations. The difference in the two operational structures relates essentially to the updating of data. In a decentralized or semi-decentralized mode of operation, the updating is operated by all nodes synchronously via an algorithmic consensus mechanism involving messaging across all nodes. This entails a slower transaction throughput than a centralized structure, although speed improvements are progressively being made. DLT may be used for an indirect CBDC architecture, as the number of transactions in wholesale payment systems is comparable with that handled by existing DLT platforms. This is also the case with wholesale CBDC platforms. Furthermore, the generally higher resilience provided by DLT is an important counterweight to issues of the slower ledger updating speed.

Given the variety of technological ways in which a system can be decentralized, it is important to note that the key characteristics of decentralized systems involve role separation and a level of trust dispersal. The Bank of England's CBDC proposal to delegate the account management role to a commercial payment interface provider (PIP,) via an application programming interface (API), is an example of (limited) decentralization via role separation (Bank of England 2021a).

In CBDC digital money systems, there are three information security properties (Brookings 2020) to be integrated within the system: confidentiality,

---

1. Oracles are algorithms using "big data" to provide a degree of trust in DLT, and especially blockchains, although, to date, the level of trust has fallen short when using accessible blockchains in real world situations.

integrity and availability. Confidentiality, ensuring that the system does not leak information to those not authorized to have access, is achieved through permissioned access to the system, either directly or via an API for previously identified clients via KYC. Integrity, with information being stored correctly and being available for audit reporting, especially in the case of system failure, by selecting a specific DLT platform which provides ease of auditing. Availability to all system participants is secured via the consensus algorithm that ensures that the copies of the data are synchronously replicated promptly at each of the vetted and identified network validators' nodes on their ledgers. This also ensures that failure of the digital ledger data records at some nodes still allows continuous payments processing across the network, in other words resilience.

Often in the literature and in descriptions of central bank projects there is some confusion as to the actual applicability of the term "blockchain" to describe the actual distributed databases being employed. To establish a definition that can encompass the variety of technology platform choices available to central banks, and whether these may be termed blockchain or DLT – and perhaps to avoid the confusion of the nomenclature used in the literature – it is worth turning to the definition of DLT provided by the Committee on Payments and Market Infrastructures:

> DLT refers to the technological infrastructure and protocols that allow *simultaneous access, validation and immutable record updating to a synchronized ledger* that is used by a network of participants that may spread across multiple entities and/or locations. In the context of payment, clearing and settlement, DLT enables entities to carry out transactions without necessarily relying on a central authority to maintain a single "golden copy" of the ledger. (CPMI 2017: 2, emphasis added).

If we add to the above highlighted descriptor of "synchronized ledger", which enables simultaneous recording, the implied descriptor of "shared ledger", then the definition would be in-line with the current usage of DLT by central banks: so that whether blockchain or DLT is used in CBDC project descriptions, the database structure used will have to meet the necessary condition of being a *shared synchronous* ledger. There will, of course, be other characteristics required of CBDC technology, as already indicated, such as cryptography. In subsequent discussion, even if the terms blockchain or DLT are used, the essential database description involves no more and no less than that of being a shared synchronous ledger, however achieved by whichever proprietary underlying database platform is used.

Blockchain

Although DLT has been around for some time, it was the advent of the use of blockchain (for a basic history, see www.stellar.org) for the development of the first and best-known cryptocurrency, Bitcoin, that sparked interest in the use of distributed database technology in the financial payments sector. The history, motivation and operation of Bitcoin has been discussed elsewhere, including by O'Neill (2021) and will not be covered here.

One important point worth making is that the permissionless feature of the Bitcoin blockchain, and some of the other early cryptocurrencies, necessitated the hermetic sealing of the blockchain, in technological terms. Trust is provided as an internal feature for the validated participants. Trust is not a feature present in any outside interaction with outside actors. There are attempts to use algorithmic approaches, utilizing past externally-generated data, to provide trust for blockchains where, necessarily, interaction with real-world organizations occurs. Solutions to the so-called "oracle" problem, providing a trusted interaction, have not achieved sufficient viability. Given the need for CBDC interaction with outside entities, trust needs to be provided elsewhere than within the blockchain database

Before discussing how the issue of trust and other aspects of DLT/blockchains relate to CBDCs, it will first be useful to define the term "blockchain" as the term is sometimes used misleadingly in descriptions of central bank CBDC projects.

Blockchain, invented in 2009, is a method for keeping data synchronized across multiple, independent stakeholders on a network. It allows the group of stakeholders, who may or may not be unrelated, and who might all have a valid reason to alter their shared data, to agree on and maintain a single dataset across the entire network. This network structure is a distributed ledger. The data is grouped into sets called "blocks". Once validated, each data block is linked or "chained" to the previous blocks to form a historical record or "blockchain", giving this distributed ledger its name. The validation of each dataset/block is made cryptographically, enabling all registered stakeholders to confirm acceptance. It is important to recognize that blockchains, unless modified, are self-contained and sealed to any participant other than those validated by "proof of work" in Bitcoin or "proof of stake" in later versions of Ethereum. Trust in these systems is embedded within the blockchain. This will clearly be a problem for CBDCs in which trust, externally measured and validated, is crucial.

In the case of a financial payments network, each payment, once transferred and validated as a correct payment between verified payers and payees across the network, is recorded and a linked historical record is formed and recorded on the ledger. (In most CBDC cases, the involvement of regulated commercial banks together with the central bank means that trust is verified outside the system, whichever database platform is used).

Versions of DLT used in some CBDC projects ensure that the DLT/blockchain database platform is situated beneath an application programming interface (API), which is the public interface for users and is controlled by the central bank. Hence only the central bank issuance and recording of transactions is on the DLT/blockchain ledger. The eCNY (PBOC 2021b), most probably, and the eNAIRA (Kedem 2021) are two such projects.

Blockchain performance issues

As suggested above, a major issue for central banks' use of full blockchain is that trust is provided as an internal feature for the validated participants. Given the need for CBDC interaction with outside entities, trust needs to be provided elsewhere than within the blockchain database. The relevant international standards, listed by ISO TC307 WG5 TS23635, indicate that DLT and blockchain systems governance "involves an approach comprising elements of central and decentral decision rights, where the accountability is situated within the network and where incentives are provided to reach consensus" (ISO TC 307). This "internalization" of accountability and trust raises the issue of interoperability between blockchains, given that CBDCs are choosing different blockchains as their preferred database platforms in the various projects. However, interoperability is a more general problem affecting the wider use of DLT, rather than simply blockchains.

The standards also recognize three broad types of blockchains:

1. Public permissionless blockchains of which Bitcoin and Ethereum cryptocurrencies/assets are examples. These "pure" blockchains are not usable by central banks without significant modification.
2. Private permissioned blockchains (with a central notarized control). These may be useful for central banks for "proof of concept" and regulatory "sandbox" experimentation. The Swedish Riksbank e-Krona and the Bank of Thailand Inthanon projects are examples.
3. Public permissioned blockchains (with some oversight of the network) in which the number of participants involved is larger than the private blockchains, so these networks are often termed consortium permissioned blockchains. These networks are the basis for several of the central banks' current pilots and prototypes of CBDC, for instance the m-CBDC Bridge project, with the central bank providing the network oversight.

Despite the constraints presented by blockchains themselves for use in retail CBDC applications, blockchains do exhibit three essential structural characteristics that explain why it was used to inform the application of DLT in the financial sector and by central banks: a form of decentralized, distributed ledger technology; use of cryptographic techniques; and the establishment and management of consensus algorithms. These characteristics enable security, resilience, traceability, transparency, anonymity and immutability, all of which are of interest to central banks in connection with the deployment of digital currencies for payments systems.

However, the drawbacks of blockchain (such as lack of scalability and poor latency) – and especially the trust issue – are the reason why an unmodified blockchain approach is unlikely to be adopted (Kudrycki 2020). CBDC database platforms are thus either restricted to utilizing the positive and beneficial characteristics of blockchains or are built from the bottom-up as a bespoke blockchain/distributed database. This approach was adopted by the R3 Corda platform. Other approaches involve specific tailoring/supplementing of the blockchain, as with the Hyperledger approaches.

Whatever technological architecture is chosen by central banks, given the potential for abuse of digital money provided by CBDCs to non-financial corporations or private citizens, it seems likely that some measure of central control over currency issuance and transactions will be retained by central banks and hence regulatory authorities.

Even if the term "blockchain" can be misleading, the problem of a lack of interoperability between all shared, synchronous database platforms remains a problem, in other words across DLT used for CBDCs. The issue arises specifically with cross-border CBDC networks that will need to communicate across differing networks to enable transactions to be managed effectively. The interoperability problems arise from the use of different encryption algorithms, consensus algorithms, digital signature schemes, hashing algorithms, transaction structures and block sizes. Given the importance of the issue it is worth mentioning one proprietary initiative, Quant's Overledger, that appears to promise the type of interoperability required and is already working with the main commercial DLT/blockchain providers, discussed in the next section, and is involved in a major Latin American CBDC project.

Overledger is described on a UK government website (Gov.UK Digital Market Place 2021, no page) as "a cloud-based Enterprise DLT operating system, that connects to many DLTs and other API based systems. It exposes their combined functionality through a single API and allows coordinated transactions and business processes to happen across all the connected DLTs and API based systems". Essentially, the Quant gateway is one protocol that *could* provide interoperability for various types of distributed ledger technology applications that may be used for CBDCs.

The Inter-American Development Bank (IDB) LACChain CBDC framework project (Allende *et al.* 2022) involves several Latin American countries. The project is supported by Overledger, enabling foreign and/or local currency to be transferred between the countries in a simple but secure manner. The pilot phase of the LACChain project is already well advanced, and full commercial development and scaling is expected to begin in 2022.

Another performance issue is that of poor transaction speeds. For example, Hyperledger Fast Fabric processes transactions at 20,000 transactions per second (TPS), whereas Visa can process transactions at 65,000 TPS.

Commercial technology choices for central banks

Currently, as can be seen from the central bank projects across the world, there are three main DLT/blockchain technology offerings from suppliers, two of which are open source and the other being proprietary: Hyperledger (open source), Corda (open source), Quorum/Ethereum (Consensys). A fourth associated technology system is Inter-ledger (Ripple), which also offers a bridge between its distributed ledger, to facilitate currency exchange, using Ripple's own intermediate currency, XRP. A fifth system, now being explored by BITT, the technology company behind (although not deployed in) the retail CBDCs in the Bahamas and Nigeria, is Stellar. Stellar is a not-for-profit organization. Other systems are likely to emerge, but first movers in new technologies tend to maintain their advantages.

The Ethereum, Quorum and Ripple protocols are based on accounts and balances. The balances are variable and change with every transaction and are achieved by the traditional transfer of debits and credits within the ledger (Zellweger-Gutknecht 2019). However, the protocols underlying Hyperledger and Corda (as for Bitcoin) are based on tokens. Unlike account balances, tokens represent an arbitrarily fixed amount of money (cash). Once established, however, the token's value never changes, like a banknote or a coin. Again, the tokens, representing cash, are transferred across the nodes of the ledger. (Nonetheless, these digital (virtual) tokens are not the same as bank notes or coins). Tokens can represent financial objects as well as cash, such as securities.

The two bespoke blockchains most often used by central banks in projects are Corda and Hyperledger, although Ethereum is also used (see the Australian Project Dunbar). Corda is a useful example of some of the key DLT operational issues involved: it uses known, trusted partner identities (at the nodes) to inject trust into the system and keeps transactions private between interacting parties, a clear goal for central banks. This structure also maintains data consistency, with the scalability to handle a high volume of transactions.

The Corda database technology illustrates the reasons why in the use of a semi-decentralized approach it is essential to provide rule-based validation of transactions and the unique finalization of transactions: two crucial aspects required for financial transactions involving the central bank issuance of fiat currency, including the associated, subsequent transactions between commercial banks.

Developed by R3 (Hearn & Gendal Brown 2019), Corda is an underlying permissioned DLT technical platform, resting on a decentralized peer-to-peer network of computer nodes, and designed specifically for highly regulated business environments, especially financial services. It operates on a need-to-know basis with data shared only between the counterparties of a transaction. Communications at a protocol level are invisible to uninvolved members of the platform. Yet observer nodes can be deployed to view transaction data, aiding compliance with legal and regulatory requirements. Corda's consensus model is based on validation and uniqueness. In the validation process each counterparty independently confirms that the transaction adheres to the shared agreed business rules. Corda uses a notary node to ensure transaction uniqueness by signing and time-stamping the transaction, avoiding double-spending. Corda's privacy design avoids use of large-scale computing resources, keeping energy consumption to a level comparable with that of conventional database applications.

Whether this semi-decentralized platform structure should be considered a blockchain is doubtful. The R3 consortium, who designed Corda, suggests (as indicated above in Hearn & Gendal Brown) that its approach should rather be described as a shared ledger in order to avoid the blockchain property of all transaction data on the ledger being communicated to all other participants on the ledger, with *all* participants confirming the data. For the participating commercial banks (or other privileged financial agents) this would raise privacy concerns and scalability issues.

Clearly, Corda has some of the key elements of blockchain technology: cryptography, transaction digital signing and smart contracts, but is not strictly a blockchain. Nonetheless, it meets the definition of DLT given by the CPMI. All the transactions that take place on the shared ledger are governed by smart contracts, which define the transactions that are allowed and who can action them. Hence, if a transaction is not signed by all of the participating parties, then it is not valid and it will not be processed. This contractual process represents the achievement of consensus.

Two other important elements of the Corda approach are a firewall that permits connections only from Corda nodes that are legitimately identified, and the ability (problematic for standard blockchains) to access and print reports from an associated relational database. Corda (see Project Jura) also enables an "observer node" to be used by the central banks to monitor and reconcile the transaction settlements via the wholesale CBDCs.

The other competing DLT/blockchain databases have corresponding mechanisms to achieve the necessary central bank/commercial bank desiderata for semi-decentralized platforms involving shared and synchronous ledgers. The advantage that Corda has had is that it was developed using a bottom-up design within a large community of banks and other financial institutions.

Smart contracts and programmability

Smart contracts, first proposed in 1994, have the terms of agreement between seller and buyer directly written into lines of code. Although in use before blockchain (for trading complex derivative contracts) they can also be triggered and executed automatically across a decentralized, distributed blockchain network. The code controls the execution, time, locations, amounts of goods or services, payments and any other contractual conditions; the transactions are irreversible, transparent and trackable. They cover delivery versus payment (DvP) and payments versus payment (PvP) transactions. These processes are programmable and can be implemented on a single platform. Hence, the efficiency of existing payment transfer processes can be improved considerably by enabling real-time payments and the integration of delivery and payment. The current time required for securities settlement, including the payment (DvP) can only be reduced to a minimum of two days. Use of the distributed technology achieves instant settlement.

This overall approach could also be applied between the central bank and commercial banks and other trusted financial intermediaries in connection with CBDC payments. Further in the future, the wider dissemination of CBDC to non-financial corporates would facilitate similar payment improvements in international business supply networks where, despite delivery of components, say from China to the UK in one day, the sterling payment can take several days or longer. With the development of the "Internet of Things"[2] speeding up these payments via a digital currency, utilizing smart programmable contracts, may become imperative.

Nonetheless, there are still problems to resolve in the areas of privacy, confidentiality and security. These problems arise partly because of the complexity of the transactions involved, which may require multiple linked product parts to be transmitted, including alternatives, with price variations. Transactions may involve more than one supplier and/or recipient in a given contract. There will

---

2. The Internet of Things (IoT) describes a network of physical objects – "things" – that are embedded with sensors, software, and other technologies, for the purpose of connecting and exchanging data with other devices and systems, over the internet.

be a requirement for encryption of transaction data and contracts to be applied, with zero-knowledge proofs – an encryption scheme whereby one party (the prover) can prove the truth of specific information to another party (the verifier) without disclosing any additional information – also required, as verification of encrypted transactions, though dependent on the complexity involved such probabilistic cryptographic proofs may not be sufficient (Enwood 2021).

CBDC design options and technology platform choices

In their pursuit of CBDCs central banks want to achieve privacy and public trust; substantial resilience against soft- and hardware failures and hacking; optimum operational performance in terms of high speed and low costs; and legal certainty and finality. Nothing less than what consumers themselves would expect from a monetary system in relation to payments in terms of convenience, functionality and security. The public expect transfers to be low-cost, fast and safe for domestic and for cross-border scenarios. Other important features are anonymity, privacy and availability, resilience and security, convenience and simple operation, in addition to off-line payments. These customer/central bank requirements will need a suitable CBDC design and a corresponding technology for delivery (Auer & Böhme 2020). As we discussed in Chapter 2, there are four design options and enabling technology choices for CBDCs: direct provision by central banks themselves; a hybrid token/account-based system; an intermediated account-based system; and indirect provision.

Direct retail CBDC

The direct model would entail the central bank itself operating the payment system, by offering retail services directly to consumers and maintaining the ledger of all such retail transactions with the CBDC involving a direct claim on the central bank. In this system the digital token asset is equivalent to a banknote; it is digital money.

The technology required for such a system would be either centralized or permissioned DLT allowing for token-based issue direct to consumers via their e-wallets. If a centralized ledger system is preferred then it would be possible – as is being explored by the Bank of England – to have an API superimposed on top of the ledger and maintained by an independent software company on behalf of the central bank (IBM 2022). The API would enable the transactions to take place without exposing any sensitive data or restricting access to authorized users, such as the API used by PayPal.

The central banks, however, may not want to expand their computing or operational capacity to cope with the increased volume of transactions, resulting from potentially millions of customers accessing and requiring the CBDC tokens. To circumvent this, they could contract with multiple private providers to supply the computing capacity, on demand, avoiding an increase in central banks' computing infrastructure and transactional activity. However, the direct CBDC model also raises specific issues relating to security and the availability of access to the digital currency (money) stored in the e-wallets.

Under this model each user would be given a private cryptographic key for authentication. The key confirms that the user has the right to transact in the digital currency concerned. How securely users can manage their keys is a question for consideration. There is evidence from cryptocurrency usage that secure and reliable storage has presented a serious challenge. Lost private keys account for an estimated 4 million Bitcoins, valued in tens of billions of US dollars being lost (Roberts & Rapp 2017).

The most likely operational system for a direct token-based CBDC design option would be in the form of a digital e-wallet, saved as an app on a mobile device. However, problems will still arise in the event of the loss, breakage, malfunction or hacking of the device. There is, unfortunately, no way that complete security can be achieved, without compromising the availability of access. The user needs both, but availability of access means some degree of insecurity.

Assuming digital-user access, with an accepted level of security, another security issue presents itself, namely validation of transactions between one user and another. The user will initiate the transaction by sending an authenticated message about the transaction to be made. This authentication involves the CBDC issuer (central bank) ensuring that the initiating user is who they say they are and similarly that the recipient user is the one nominated, and, finally, that if a payment is made that it is made once only on its ledger.

In a typical online banking system, the user authentication and the transaction authentication are simultaneously validated. This can be achieved because the issuer of the private money (the bank) is the same institution that authenticates the initiating transaction user. In the direct CBDC system the central bank issued the public money, but it needs also to ensure that the initiating user is who they say they are.

In the Bahamas, Island Pay – the Bahamian technology company which enables users to pay in Sand Dollars at merchants, via its digital currency mobile wallet – issues a new Bahamas Sand Dollar prepaid card as a supplement to its mobile phone wallet app. The company will combine its technology platform with Mastercard's merchant network and technology platform to reduce the operational cash distribution costs across the islands. The Island Pay card thus allows users to instantly convert the Bahamas Sand Dollar CBDC to traditional

Bahamian dollars to spend on goods and services anywhere Mastercard is accepted within the Bahamian territory.

Hybrid token/account-based

In a hybrid CBDC model, the payment system operation is divided between the customer/client and the commercial bank. The commercial bank (or other financial intermediary) manages the retail transactions, on behalf of the client whose digital wallet account they hold. The central bank is responsible for keeping a ledger recording the retail transactions, with again a direct claim by the client on the central bank involved. The technology required for this system can be either a centralized database or a permissioned, distributed ledger database, allowing for account or token-based digital money issue to the client, via their e-wallets held by their bank.

The solutions to the security and availability problems of the direct model may be a little easier to resolve in a hybrid system, although solutions will still be required, via cooperation with the commercial banks and other financial intermediaries. The problem is one of scale in relation to the data storage and management requirements of millions of customers and billions and trillions of transactions. For example, China now has 140 million users of its e-CNY and 10 million corporate accounts have been created, according to Mu Changchun (of the PBOC). The volume of transactions totalled 150 million, worth ¥62 billion ($9.7 billion) in trials across a dozen regions (Mu 2021). Digital yuan operators can open four types of e-wallets for customers. The least privileged only requires a phone number, so would be anonymous even to the PBOC. Daily transaction values for this type of e-wallet holder are capped at ¥5,000, with an annual cap of ¥50,000 ($7,200). The highest privileged e-wallet would need to be opened at a bank counter with personal identification, with no transaction cap. Mu reiterated (Mu 2021) that these e-wallets would collect less transaction information than traditional digital payment services. The PBOC would not provide the information to any third-party or other government agencies unless stipulated by law.

Given the desire of China's central bank to maintain central surveillance of all e-CNY transactions, they have tailored the model accordingly, although it should be noted that the smallest, least privileged accounts will remain anonymous, being accessed via a phone number only. The computing power deployed by the PBOC appears sufficient to handle the number of retail transactions, to date. Its wider extension, to potentially 1,000 times more customers, is a task of considerably greater magnitude. For the central bank to keep such a data record of billions/trillions of retail customer transactions represents a staggering challenge. It is not yet clear precisely how the PBOC and/or the Chinese state will move forward to achieve this level of operational performance. Under this model the management of the retail transactions underpinning will be handled by the Chinese state banks and other financial intermediaries, such as Alipay and WeChat Pay.

The specifics of blockchain/distributed ledger database platform underpinning the e-CNY is not publicly available. The PBOC document of July 2021 (Mu 2021) offers some general indication, but no more:

> The e-CNY system adopts a distributed and platform-based design, which enhances the resilience and expansibility of the system and supports the rapid growth in the volume of e-CNY transactions. To ensure the reliability and soundness of the system, the PBOC uses a mix of technologies such as trusted computing and special encryption based on hardware and software integration. The PBOC also builds up multi-layer security systems and design a data center solution featuring multisite high availability and 24/7 non-stop services, thus guaranteeing city-level disaster tolerance and business continuity.
>
> The e-CNY system combines centralized architecture with distributed architecture, forming a hybrid technical framework featuring the co-existence of dual states, namely, steady state and agile state, as well as the integrated development of centralized and distributed architectures. (Mu 2021: 10–11)

This two-layered approach, involving an API to leave public access beyond the underlying DLT/blockchain database platform, is likely to be favoured by several central banks. It is the current approach of the Bank of England. The aim is to achieve resilience and scalability. As with China's system, the commercial banks and other financial intermediaries/payment system providers will be responsible for managing the retail transactions. The approach can be run with an account-based system as well as tokens.

The publicly revealed plans or explorations of several central banks (including the Bank of England) focus on two-layer CBDC architectures, namely an account-based system. Existing financial intermediaries, commercial banks and payment service providers are all classified in the architecture as "payment interface providers" (PIPs). These constitute a second layer on top of the CBDC, divided by an API, and serve as the main interface between users and the underlying DLT ledger of the CBDC, controlled by the central bank. Two-layer architectures align closely with current customer service delivery models and compliance mechanisms for countering the funding of terrorism (AML/CFT).

Although nominally two layers, there are effectively three layers. The first two layers are the CBDC secure core-ledger base layer accessed only by the central bank, and the private API access layer which allows financial intermediaries, commercial banks, and payment service providers to connect to the core ledger. A final, external layer allows users, customers or merchants to register to use the digital money payment system via a user-friendly interface provided by the payment service providers themselves. Generally, this layered system would provide a high degree of privacy, albeit not the same as that provided by banknotes. Moreover, the system may evolve into one in which the PIPs deploy programmable smart contracts for business customers, but then there is a danger that systemic risks could escape the observation and control of regulators. The establishment by the central bank of common technical and operating interface standards would seem necessary.

Intermediated account-based

In this model private sector financial intermediaries, principally commercial banks, manage the retail transactions of the digital money customer, in relation to their digital-money account. They maintain the ledger containing a record of all retail transactions. The central bank maintains a central ledger of corresponding wholesale transactions, matching the retail activity. It will be the responsibility of the financial intermediary to ensure the correspondence of retail and wholesale transactions requirements. There continues to be a direct CBDC claim of the client on the central bank and the relationship between the commercial bank or financial intermediary and the client is a custodial one. This relationship has implications for the technology choice to be made, involving the precise operational and legal relationship between the commercial bank or financial intermediary and the client.

Insofar as the "digital wallet" now takes the form of an account with a commercial bank or other regulated financial intermediary, it does not need to be accessed via a software application. Hence, a two-tier CBDC architecture may be used, in which the bank or intermediary holding the account interfaces with the customer and can activate and record transactions on behalf of its authenticated customer, as is the case with current internet banking practice.

A technological structure that allows intermediaries to vouch for the authenticity of users' transactions has the benefit of conceptual and design simplicity, but there are drawbacks. For instance, if the financial intermediary's software system is hacked – rather than a simple (though effective) denial of service – then potentially all clients are at risk of forged transactions. It may be that lessons can be learned from account-based cryptocurrencies. Ethereum, for example, uses a cryptographic public key, which works with a corresponding user's private key, to ensure the validity of any individual transactions. Only these valid transactions are then recorded on the distributed ledger. Hence, whichever financial intermediary's choice of decentralized ledger system is used for the retail CBDC, it will be preferable for a matching cryptographic key system to be employed to preserve security of transactions. If this model is chosen, then it is likely that this method of protecting retail transactions at the level of the financial intermediary will be mandatory. Moreover, such a protection would be in the interests of the commercial bank or financial intermediary, as it is they who will, conceivably be the subject of any legal claim from their customer.

Indirect provision/account-based

When the system is based on indirect provision, there is no direct CBDC claim on the central bank. Instead the claim on the central bank is by the intermediaries, who also manage and record all retail transactions. It could be argued that as this variant does not permit any direct claim on the central bank, it should not be regarded as a CBDC, but this seems unreasonable as it is still issued directly to the commercial bank on behalf of the customer. Moreover, the definition of a retail CBDC by CPMI (see BIS 2020) defines a retail CBDC as any claim on the central bank that is different from the current system of wholesale account claims (see also Bech & Garratt 2017)

All retail transactions management, recording and claims on the digital accounts are the responsibility of the banks and financial intermediaries. However, these intermediary liabilities to their retail customers, as in current practice, are backed with claims on the central bank. In this model, the custodial relationship of the commercial bank and the client is most obvious. The bank customer will not notice any significant difference from their current relationship with the bank, except that they will have a public digital money account, in addition to any private money accounts.

For the central bank, because the role of the bank is limited to the recording of a relatively few wholesale transactions, it would be possible to use a DLT platform. The experience of central banks in pursuing the use of DLT for cross-border financial asset transfers may eventually facilitate its use in this indirect design model.

Regulatory liability network: technology considerations

Before discussing the technology issues surrounding wholesale CBDC/cross-border payments architecture, it will be useful to examine the financial market infrastructure containing an innovative conceptual design for a retail CBDC (involving a new and challenging definition of "sovereign money"). The design concept of the regulatory liability network (RLN) has been suggested by a consortium of banks and others, including Citi, OCBC, Goldman Sachs, Barclays, BondeValue, Bank of America, Bank of New York, Payoneer, Paypal, Wells Fargo, SETL and Linklaters. The conceptual monetary policy issues raised by the proposal, with the addition of, admittedly regulated, stablecoin issuers to the commercial banks as equivalent private money issuers, were detailed in Chapter 2. In the following, the data structure of the proposal is outlined. The technology that would be involved raises wider issues.

Tokens would be issued by any of the three regulated institutions, not, as now, by the central bank only, and would represent claims on the specific individual issuer. Digital wallets or accounts would only be available to clients following strict KYC identity checks. Payment transfers between the participating institutions work by extinguishing liabilities of the sender and creating matching liabilities on the receiving side. Final settlement is achieved only via central bank liabilities in tokens between all participants. The RLN would be a new financial market infrastructure (FMI) and would be the application layer run on top on a modified distributed ledger database platform, in a decentralized fashion. The database framework would require partitioning within the larger data set so that each partitioned segment records the liabilities of each participating institution, in their own proprietary software. The RLN would also be able to accommodate other assets from the regulated entities, such as sovereign or corporate bonds, across a global network.

However, would the monetary architecture envisaged be technologically feasible and practicable? R3 has suggested that its DLT architecture and operational structure would be capable of handling the conceptual design of the RLN, although it would require considerable work to ensure that it was feasible and practicable:

> The proposed RLN payments procedure is already supported by the R3 sandbox architecture. The reason is that Corda is built in such a way that transactions between two nodes are not visible to other nodes. Each node has its own subset of the ledger that only shows the transactions in which the node has participated. In addition, there is a notary service which verifies that there is no double spending of liabilities (possible fraud) by one of the parties. This existing setup already meshes seamlessly with the RLN concept. [...]
>
> The reason that multiple issuers is feasible in the existing sandbox framework is because the proposed RLN incorporates multiple partitions, one for each regulated participant. Partitioning in programming

refers to a logical division of a larger data set. In the same way each RLN partition belongs to a different regulated entity, all of whom contribute to the global population of regulated liabilities. The liabilities of each participant are recorded in their partition, which is their own territory as if they were recording liabilities on their own proprietary systems (R3 2022a).

Nonetheless, the RLN concept is presented as "technology neutral". Although it would probably require implementation via some form of distributed ledger or blockchain to implement its operational framework. There are several variables to be considered, such as whether the distributed ledger system would be permissioned and public, or permissioned and private. The former is unlikely, and the system would most likely need to be a permissioned consortium. The auditing of the system would be another issue, relating to how and where in the system the transactions data is recorded. These issues need to be considered in any use of DLT in relation to CBDCs.

Cross-border payments

Although both retail or wholesale CBDCs can be used in facilitating cross-border payments, the current thinking and policy direction among central banks, evidenced by the projects they are working on, is leaning towards using wholesale CBDCs (wCBDCs), via the cross-border integration of RTGS systems, as indicated by the BIS m-CBDC Bridge prototyping project, Project Dunbar and Project Jura.

Prototyping and piloting in this context involve the use of DLT to facilitate cross-border payments, involving multiple currencies. The three main proprietary DLT databases that have been tested in the context of the pilot and prototyping projects are Corda, Hyperledger and Ethereum. There appears to be little doubt about the advantages of semi-decentralized databases and DLT systems for this wholesale RTGS approach for multicurrency cross-border payments. Nonetheless, further prototyping work is being undertaken before the various technical, resilience, and other operational and legal issues can be said to have been resolved. As Project Jura has demonstrated (see Appendices), in the context of actual legal and regulatory constraints, a dual currency cross-border financial payment transfer system can work successfully, both in technical and in regulatory terms.

There is a growing raft of projects taking place around the world that involve not only central banks, but also large private companies. The main advantages sought from wholesale CBDCs are the reduction of settlement time, lowered default risk, more efficient settlement of securities transactions and legal compliance. As indicated in reports on the projects Helvetia, Jura and Dunbar, the early signs appear propitious. Among wholesale CBDCs projects the ECB and the Bank of Japan have jointly piloted a blockchain-based application for the settlement of "atomic" swaps that enable simultaneous and final settlement of trading transactions (ECB 2020a).

There is the potential for unpredictable market outcomes to lead to an unwanted oligopoly in distributed ledger technology available for the public sector. A private/public sector initiative, involving IBM, HSBC and the Banque de France (IBM 2021b), apparently initiated by the latter bank in 2021, tested direct CBDC transactions in a hybrid cloud environment across both Hyperledger and Corda technology platforms. Although the initiative appears to be valuable, it could reinforce a duopoly between the two leading technology companies in this area. The project used an advanced token and digital wallet settlement capability, covering not only CBDCs, but also eBonds (delivery versus payment across primary issuance and secondary trading and coupon payments), and foreign exchange (pricing and payment versus payment settlement). Distributed ledgers based on IBM's Hyperledger Fabric and R3's Corda were integrated using IBM Research's Weaver interoperability tool. Mark Williamson, managing director GFX eRisk, Partnerships & Propositions at HSBC, said:

> We were pleased to be selected by Banque de France to conduct this exciting experiment. Our collaboration with IBM on this initiative has resulted in this milestone of streamlining front-to-back securities and foreign exchange DVP and PVP settlement processes. Interoperability across different DLT's and technologies was key is demonstrating how to save time, reduce market risk and improve security for transactions between central banks, commercial banks and in time our clients around the world. (Lomax 2021, no page)

Likhit Wagle, general manager Global Banking & Financial Markets at IBM commented that "[a]s central banks around the world begin to explore the potential for CBDC to bring greater transparency and security to financial transactions, this initiative provides a comprehensive roadmap" (Lomax 2021, no page). There is, of course, room for public/private collaboration, but such collaboration does not rule out inadvertently setting up oligopolistic situations.

There is a general question, which concerns all of the above CBDC design models, namely that of ultimate system resilience. Hence, although it is correct to suggest that CBDC modified DLT structures provide substantial resilience against technological failure, it may be argued that the availability of physical banknotes provide ultimate payment system resilience, in the case of catastrophic digital failure across part or the whole of the digitized monetary system. There are plenty of examples of government and central bank electronic systems, such as CHAPS, ECB Target 2 and Fedwire, suffering significant outages. In the, admittedly unlikely, event that there only central bank digital money was available – and with increasing examples of financial systems being the subject of private, and possible hostile state, cyber-attacks – there appears to be a need, in order to secure ultimate resilience, to provide either recourse to alternative forms of parallel private electronic payment or to the availability of cash.

A separate general issue concerns the requirement of any payment system to provide legal and final certainty that the financial transactions cannot be retroactively modified or reversed. In modern contemporary economies this finality is provided by the central banks. The issuance and use of digital money by central banks means that the cryptographic procedures – in whatever CBDC model is selected – must be foolproof. In the event of any cryptographic system failure, the ability to remedy the failure immediately must be provided.

The three extant retail CBDCs being widely piloted – in the Bahamas, Nigeria and China – are all using the direct or hybrid model, with an API-supported, tiered approach that utilizes a modified blockchain approach as the bottom layer, with the central bank firmly in charge of the programme interface protocol and able to provide the guarantee of legal finality. There appears to be every prospect that several, if not the majority, of central banks around the world may support this API technological approach to implementing retail CBDCs. There is, however, no valid reason to suppose that the other CBDC design models under consideration cannot be structured and operated in such a manner as to provide the technical and operational certainty required, and in a manner which preserves the legal finality required to fulfil the crucial societal trust in fiat money, via the supporting "trust-anchor role" of the central bank.

Currently, Corda, Hyperledger and Ethereum are the main competing databases, but there are already a variety of other databases available and more will likely come on to the market. It might be argued that the open-source nature of Corda and Hyperledger ensures competition and optimizes social welfare. However, this may not be the case. There is also a wider question concerning the impact of open-source software on innovation. It has been found (Zhou & Choudray 2021) that, perhaps surprisingly, competition from open-source software does not necessarily lead to an increase in social welfare. This research also suggests that various factors, relating to customer requirements and targeted approaches to design may be important drivers in terms of innovation and operational fit.

Conclusion

The exploration of CBDCs by central banks has been, to a significant extent, driven by the technology developed and used by the private sector, latterly in an innovative manner in respect of financial services and the monetary payments system. Although final choices for retail CBDCs have not yet been made by all central banks, the selection of some form of a semi-decentralized distributed ledger database – albeit not necessarily "full" blockchain, despite the terminology sometimes used – rather than a centralized database structure appears now to be the main option being explored. However, the public are unlikely have direct access to the DLT, but to an API layer. Certainly, DLT is the choice being made for wholesale CBDCs in a cross-border environment. Nonetheless, other forms of public permissioned blockchain structures are being explored (Allende *et al.* 2022).

Hence, given the retail CBDC model design choices, including also using either accounts or tokens, further technological choices have to be made. Insofar as tokens are involved then the central bank will issue these (as in China), seeding the database which will then be transmitted to the financial players, principally commercial banks, via APIs.

Several central banks, encouraged by the BIS, are likely to select a potential retail CBDC design choice that represents the least disruptive impact on the current wholesale digital structure of the monetary system. In relation to the sensitive area of multicurrency cross-border payments, the extension of the RTGS system, via a wholesale CBDC structure, is the preferred choice, certainly for public institutional and many commercial bank transfers. The technology choice here will be DLT, however, given the lower likelihood of linked blocks of transactions data being transferred between network nodes and other crucial considerations, it will not be full "blockchain". The likely design will involve both centralized control via an observer node and issuance of the digital currency via a central bank node, with individual transaction data messages being transmitted across the nodes. The two most likely commercial DLTs used as the underlying database for the wholesale CBDCs are Corda and Hyperledger, at least at the present time, using tokens. It is possible that for individual financial transfers, such as tourist expenditure or remittances (Nigeria), retail CBDCs may be used. China successfully piloted the use of its e-CNY retail currency for visitors to the Winter Olympics in February 2022, for example.

Notwithstanding the above indications, there are still a considerable number of security, privacy, scalability, performance, resilience, and other technology issues, to be resolved before any definitive commencement of the widespread establishment of CBDCs can be envisaged, especially in relation to retail CBDCs and the technology to be employed. An extremely innovative technology

approach – in both substantive, digital monetary terms and in database technology terms – has been put forward by the consortium of US major banks
mentioned, and others, of a tokenized, regulated liabilities network, involving
a merger of central banks, commercial banks, and other issuers of e-money
(such as stablecoins). However, this approach – leaving aside conceptual design
concerns – would require further significant technological specification to find
a suitable technology platform. This suggested innovation is indicative of the
breadth and depth of the further exploration required, especially on the technologies to be employed for CBDCs.

4
IMPACT ON THE COMMERCIAL BANKING SECTOR

The introduction of CBDCs is likely to have significant impacts on customers' use of both current and deposit accounts at commercial banks whichever of the four model design variants is implemented. The BIS "recommendation" of an intermediation model would preserve much of the current role of the commercial banks, as would the indirect model, albeit at the potential risk of losing some of the CBDC's wider benefits. Criticism has been levied at the current commercial banking system and structure and the need for reform (see RSA 2020; Lloyd 2021). Moreover, in a speech in 2021, Sir Jon Cunliffe, Deputy Governor of the Bank of England stated that "It is not the responsibility of financial stability authorities to preserve any particular business models, including in banking" (Cunliffe 2021a).

However, CBDCs are not being introduced into a monetary system where commercial banks have an effective monopoly position. Indeed, one of the reasons given for the potential introduction of CBDCs is the increasing provision of competing peer-to-peer internet-based financial payment systems, now accompanied by the introduction of stablecoins and the concerns they raise as providing competing private money channels in relation to Forex (foreign exchange transactions) and cross-border securities exchange. What appears to be clear, at this stage, is that the extent of loan creation via existing alternative finance (AFI) from payment service providers – including fintech providers such as Funding Circle – despite growing strongly, still only represents around 10 per cent of total lending in the UK (CCAF 2021).

Commercial banking: business model and existing digital money

Banks run a complicated business model, serving multiple, interrelated functions including everyday banking, loans and payments. So far, they have not been unduly disturbed by internet-based payment systems, and the share of the payments market by alternative finance provision has not been large. However, stablecoins and the potential involvement of Big Tech, may shake the complacency of the banks (Lloyd 2021). The banks' position is bolstered by their access to very large client bases and the provision of a range of relatively low cost, but also low unit-profit services, such as account administration, distribution and payment transfers. The impact of CBDCs on banks may depend on their ability to continue to provide these services, which supply useful information for credit provision to customers (Parlour *et al.* 2020). CBDC accounts operated by fintech and perhaps Big Tech companies to provide the payment services – and possibly credit services – would have a damaging impact on commercial banks.

An alternative direct investment safe-route via CBDCs may have a significant impact on banks, causing them to increase deposit rates in order to retain customers, and thereby cutting the margin between the interest on deposits and that on loans. The banks' choice then might be to increase loan rates to protect their profits, with consequential damage to business development and economic growth. The position of building societies and savings banks would be even more acute as their overall profits are partly dependent on maintaining a sufficient interest margin.

As suggested with an account-based CBDC, commercial banks may be able to act as custodians of the customer's CBDC account, as they already do for financial assets for some clients. However, if this CBDC model variant is not used then might this threaten to undermine the sustainability of existing custodian services, based on account security and trust.

The current structure of the monetary system involves the central bank, as the trust anchor of the fiat currency, working as part of a financial architecture in which commercial banks play a pivotal role. Traditionally, the maturity transformation role involves the creation of short-term, liquid liabilities to finance long-term, illiquid investments, such as small business loans. In a modern economy this is not done by creating the deposits first, but via the intervention of the central bank's creation of reserves (liabilities on central bank balance sheets) to match the loans created by the banks (assets on commercial bank balance sheets). It may be questioned, however, whether commercial banks do, in practice, provide adequate term loans to small businesses (Lloyd 2021). The advent of CBDC issuance to other financial intermediaries could provide alternative sources of loan finance for small businesses.

With the introduction of CBDC accounts, these accounts would also have access to central bank reserves, including the protection from risk and the provision of liquidity. In times of financial crisis, commercial bank deposits are generally regarded as a safe haven. Were CBDCs to destabilize the safe risk and liquidity backing of these bank deposits, and their protection by deposit insurance (in the UK limited to £85,000), then their role in the transformation of maturity in the economy may also be destabilized. Whether, and if so in what form, CBDCs should be introduced, to minimize the potential disturbance of the current system of maturity transformation and liquidity provision requires careful consideration by the central banks (Fernandez-Villaverde *et al.* 2020).

Digital money already exists in the form of the wholesale digital money system in which the central bank provides two essential elements to permit a modern monetary system to function efficiently and safely. First, it underpins the system by providing, in unlimited quantities, reserves to commercial banks. It matches the loans, recorded as assets on the commercial banks' balance sheets, by the reserves, recorded as liabilities on the central bank's balance sheet. This set of transactions allows the maturity transformation, and associated liquidity provision, to enable loans to be made to businesses for working capital and for investment, and to personal retail banking customers. The digital money is thus provided solely to regulated private financial institutions, principally commercial banks, in the wholesale financial system, rather than directly to other non-financial corporate bodies or citizens in the retail financial system. Second, the central bank's issuance of public fiat money ensures that the private commercial bank money is thereby guaranteed, and that clearance and settlement by the central bank, via its wholesale monetary actions, has finality, thereby providing the essential trust anchor of the monetary system.

The impact of CBDCs on the associated real time gross settlement (RTGS) system – by which substantial interbank payments are settled continuously and with finanality via the central bank – is one issue that will need to be addressed. The payment system is known as CHAPS (for large payments) and BACS (for smaller payments) in the UK and SEPA in the eurozone (TARGET2 is the equivalent of the RTGS system in the eurozone). The impact of the extension of digital money to directly cover individuals' transactions would be likely to lead to a vast expansion of the volume of transactions under the current RTGS system. Nonetheless, it may still be possible for RTGS to function alongside a direct retail CBDC model.

Perhaps, as importantly, for central banks and for the financial stability of that system, is the extended use of corresponding RTGS systems between countries, to settle cross-border financial transactions, in *fiat* currencies. In this way, the above w-CBDC system would provide a safe, efficient and secure cross-border payments system, using the latest available distributed (shared and synchronous) ledger system. This extension of the w-CBDC system would be likely to also involve other regulated financial intermediaries, as well as commercial banks. Notwithstanding the pivotal role played by the commercial banks in the current monetary system, they have been slow to adapt to changing circumstances, especially digitization and internal back-office operations. This situation has led to competitive pressures from challenger banks and other private payment systems, although, so far, the dominance of commercial banks has not been seriously challenged (Lloyd 2021).

CBDCs and the commercial banking system

As many studies have found (Independent Commission on Banking 2011) there is a high level of inertia exhibited by customers to switch banks, as challenger banks have discovered, especially in the small and medium-sized business sector. Commercial banks provide a high degree of security and trust for clients. For many customers the net performance of the commercial banks (despite occasional serious "glitches" and failures) is acceptable without signs of any significant customer "desertion". Alternative finance, especially in the US with the introduction of stablecoins, has pointed in their marketing materials to flaws in the service provided by banks: customers share personal data that is vulnerable to security breaches; clearing and settlement of cross-border transactions can take several days; the hours of operation are limited with physical branches being closed down at an increasing rate. Moreover, a significant proportion of the population (around 5 million in the UK) are either unbanked or underbanked and unable to access certain financial services, such as overdrafts or competitive credit cards (Rowlington & McKay 2016). Alternative finance providers offer options – especially with decentralized finance and internet-based services – to remedy the earlier defects of traditional banks. So far, these attempts have not been notably successful, although for less risk-averse, large potential business customers, and the financially savvy young, stablecoins may become attractive.

Commercial bank charges for transaction services reflect their monopoly position, and the same could be said for the major credit card companies. There are reforms underway in the UK, EU and US. There are attempts in the UK, via the Forum of the Payment Systems Regulator (PSR 2021) – a subsidiary of the Payment Systems Regulator (PSR) – to replace the current split architecture between BACS (bankers automatic clearing system) and the Faster Payments Service by a single purpose-built architecture, ensuring that the UK's retail interbank payments system is "future-proofed", as payments technology and people's habits continue to evolve. The aim is for the new platform to allow new and existing payment service companies to develop services that benefit consumers and businesses using the system. However, there has been criticism of the slow and narrowed development of new payments architecture (NPA). It should be noted that, currently, Mastercard runs the infrastructure for BACS, Faster Payments and LINK through its subsidiary Vocalink, owned by the UK commercial banks.

A useful, if critical, commentary of the Byzantine operation of the attempt to establish the NPA is given by Lyddon (2021, no page):

> PSR has dictated that the major UK banks should divest themselves of Vocalink, because of the market dominance of those banks over UK payments. Under the PSR's intended "layered market model" there should be several separate marketplaces for layers like infrastructure provision, payment scheme management, settlement, and provision of payment services to end-users. No one market actor should have a dominant market share of any one layer, and ideally each layer should contain its own set of market actors, competing with one another for the business of the actors in the layers above and below This has back-fired as well: UK payments now has an actual duopoly in the shapes of Mastercard and Visa, who were already strongly positioned in more than one layer before the PSR was created and who have benefitted enormously from the move to online shopping during the pandemic, from the switch from cash to card, and from digitalization in general.

Missing from the projected NPA at this stage are CHAPS, and apparently also LINK, Visa and Mastercard. Both Mastercard and Visa are themselves payment systems regulated by the PSR. Although Lyddon's criticism about the role of the two credit card companies may appear harsh, the layers of bureaucracy involved in the reform process may have led to a less than rigorous pursuance of radical reform – the PSF is a subsidiary of the PSR, which is itself a subsidiary of the FCA – and justify his concerns.

Notwithstanding these issues, familiar in UK IT systems procurement, Faster Payments has achieved significant increases in volumes processed (PSR 2020). The SIPS (single immediate payments) volume of transactions increased by almost 30 per cent in the first six months of 2021 from the 2020 figure of 2.3 billion transactions per second. However, there is little doubt that, not only in the UK, but also in the EU and the US, the impact of operating in an increasingly digital world is creating considerable technological and operational challenges for the commercial banking sector (see Lloyd 2021: 83–94).

Across the US and Europe, a collaboration was announced between the US Clearing House, which operates the US real time payments network, and CHIPS the US dollar clearance system, EBA Clearing, a provider of pan-European payment-infrastructure technology, and the financial-messaging specialist SWIFT. Founded in 1998, EBA Clearing is owned by 48 of the major banks operating in Europe and is based on a country-neutral governance model. EBA Clearing manages and operates the payment services EURO1, STEP1, STEP2 and RT1. Both EURO1 and STEP2 have been classified as systemically important payment systems (SIPS) by the European Central Bank. RT1, the first pan-European re-al-time payment system, went live in 2017 and processes euro instant payments complying with the European Payments Council's SEPA Instant Credit Transfer Scheme. In 2021, EBA Clearing launched R2P, a request to pay messaging infra-structure service.

In October 2021 the consortium completed a proof-of-concept aimed at introducing faster cross-border payments (Lucas 2021). Currently these cross-border payments can take hours and sometimes days to complete. The pilot demonstrated that existing regional instant-payment systems can be leveraged for cross-border payments, applicable to financial institutions of all sizes as a solution for speedy cross-border payments, without having to build or connect to a separate network. The initiative used the latest messaging standard ISO 20022, aimed at encouraging enhanced cross-border payment systems. In terms of implementation the focus of the three companies (and their members) will focus on the US–euro currency corridor.

Irrespective of CBDCs, there are attempts to improve the efficiency of current payment systems. A report on the implications of digitization for the future of banking and for macroprudential policy was published in January 2022 by the Academic Scientific Committee (ASC) of the European Systemic Risk Board (ESRB), in which the ASC considered three scenarios for the EU financial system in 2030. In the first scenario incumbent commercial banks continue their dominance; in the second, incumbent commercial banks retrench; and in the third commercial banks operate in a monetary environment in which central banks issue digital currencies. They then looked at the implications of each for an EU macroprudential policy response. One problem that the study (Beck *et al.* 2022) acknowledges is that the scenarios are endogenous to the (unknown) regulatory environment over the next ten years, and hence are likely to be modified. A further problem is that the first two scenarios omit CBDCs entirely, which is unrealistic given the current level of central bank interest in them. Given the likelihood of the less "radical" CBDC options being selected for implementation by governments and central banks, the commercial banks are likely to retain a role in any monetary system going forward. The second commercial bank scenario involves a substantial retrenchment of the commercial banking sector in favour of a substantial increase in fintech and big tech companies in the financial sector (albet likely concentrating on payment systems). As a scenario, given the inevitable problems of shared macroprudential and microprudential policy supervision between the EU and member states (made even more problematic if regulation of cryptocurrencies is involved; see discussion of the MICA Directive in Chapter 1), the EU would probably want to avoid this eventuality.

Commercial bank reaction to CBDCs

Around 2014, during the early interest in CBDCs, the perception of commercial banks in Europe and in the US, was that the exploration of this area of monetary innovation would be unlikely to disturb, in the short to medium-term, the substantial retail banking market, which commercial banks dominated (ING 2021). The monetary architecture broadly satisfied customer requirements, and major challenges from new fast financial payment providers had not materialized, despite increasing use of the internet and digital technology. Although wholesale CBDCs were beginning to be examined by central banks for cross-border payments, those changes seemed not to impinge significantly on the retail banking area.

Since 2020, this complacency has given way to an awakening concern, prompted by the advent of stablecoins and the lack of consistent regulation governing them and other cryptocurrencies. Commercial banks are now engaging in the discussions around CBDCs, and some are involved in proof of concept and pilot projects. They are also, as evidenced by some of the commercial banks' participation in the House of Lords enquiry, starting to emphasize the risks of retail CBDCs (House of Lords 2022). Assuming central banks introduce some form of retail CBDC in the medium term, commercial banks may have to turn to lobbying for the CBDC design model that is the least disruptive of the current monetary system and for regulation of stablecoin and the alternative finance sector.

Increasingly, contact with banks is already via mobile phone apps. Currently, it is not clear how exactly the customer interface requirements will manifest themselves in CBDCs. Hence, planning may need to encompass the potential hosting of electronic wallets and sending tokens on behalf of customers with authenticated proof of identity. The customer experience will have to be as simple as possible, consistent with security and privacy. Eventually, CBDC transactions may well need to become programmable with smart contracts, especially for commercial clients. The aim should be to be able to offer a seamless and secure international payments ecosystem for the bank's clients.

More generally, banks need to recognize a variety of issues in their forward planning, namely new approaches to processing payments; new supply-chain possibilities for payments; integration with new decentralized systems; and a new portfolio of banking services. Close consultation between commercial banks and central banks will be critical to determining the roles of banks in the new monetary digital infrastructure as any CBDC is likely to be a public–private partnership. Nonetheless, commercial banks should be prepared for a future in which the provision of private digital money may not be restricted to commercial banks, as is effectively the case now. Other payment service providers, including stablecoin issuers may be authorized to offer CBDC services, in relation to both retail and, possibly, wholesale CBDCs.

Notwithstanding a new, more competitive future scenario, it seems likely that the strength of commercial banks KYC expertise may still allow them to fulfil a crucial intermediary role between central banks, non-banks and end-users. This role may give rise to opportunities for commercial banks to provide new, potentially chargeable services.

Disintermediation

The launch of a CBDC may lead to a level of disintermediation and loss of deposit accounts, and possible knock-on effects on loan interest charges and liquidity. If CBDCs are viewed principally as an asset to hold and, if the asset demand is significant enough to disturb funding markets for non-financial corporations and banks themselves, then a CBDC may substitute for other assets currently offered by non-financial corporations as collateral or by banks in repo-markets.[1] This might lead to banks holding less-liquid assets to accommodate the impacts of CBDC issuance. Additionally, a CBDC could increase competition from non-banks receiving more payments via CBDCs and reducing the banks' own payment-related income streams (a point made in Chapter 2). If, as seems likely, CBDCs are not introduced as interest-bearing assets, then they may be regarded primarily as substitutes for cash and not as competition to deposit accounts. Customers would be more likely to use CBDCs to cover normal day-to-day spending needs with it forming a transactional payment mechanism and not being a store of value and, hence potentially, competitive with commercial banks deposits. In any event the central bank will have control over the volume of issuance, and by limiting the amount issued, in any given period, would also be able to reduce the impact of the digital money.

A similar negative impact could also occur if the central bank itself entered into the payments market, although this seems unlikely in developed economies. For central banks, retail payments would involve an entirely new activity, requiring expertise they do not have and costs they will not wish to incur.

There may also be some impacts on increased competition for payments from existing non-bank payment providers. Moreover, commercial banks are themselves investing in digitization of their payment systems to strengthen their competitive position. Although it would be wrong to ignore disintermediation

---

1. Repo markets involve trading (usually overnight) between cash and short-term government securities (usually Treasury bills) and are used by central banks to ensure the interest rate they set remains within a narrow range.

as a potentially undesirable consequence of CBDC introduction, non-interest-bearing CBDCs and the desire of the central banks to continue a partnership with the commercial banks are likely reasons for amelioration of any significant disintermediation.

In January 2022, the Economic Affairs Committee of the House of Lords published their report (House of Lords 2022), which took a negative view overall about CBDCs, suggesting that they represented "a solution looking for a problem". They were especially concerned about the potential of CBDCs to lead to significant disintermediation of the UK's commercial banks. The concern is that a proportion of customers may wish to transfer money out of their existing bank accounts into their CBDC wallets. This action would weaken the balance sheets of the commercial banks and increase the size of the central bank's balance sheet. The uncertainty about the level of disintermediation is extreme. A Canadian National Bank study in November 2021 (Li 2021) suggested that the percentage moved from commercial banks accounts to CBDC accounts could range between 4 per cent and 52 per cent, depending on whether customers regard CBDC accounts as being closer to cash or to deposits. The Bank of England provided their "illustrative scenario" of a possible 20 per cent level of disintermediation, roughly the total of uninsured deposits:

> We have modelled a very prudent assumption, which is that 20 per cent of the deposit base in the banking system could move out of the banking system into central bank digital money in some form or other. That roughly represents all the uninsured deposits. Looking at it another way, we tried to look at the behavioural response if people had an extreme preference for safety and the like. It is a pretty prudent assumption that 20 per cent of household and corporate transactional deposits move to CBDC. (Cunliffe 2021a)

The BoE's analysis backing this scenario and its underpinning assumptions is not only complex and multifaceted but implies an unrealistic level of sophistication – and assumed average levels of deposit account (as opposed to current accounts) – of the general public, both personal and corporate. It is difficult to know how much credence to place on this illustrative figure. On the other hand, as suggested below and confirmed by Cunliffe, the deputy governor, in his evidence to the House of Lords, it is highly likely that banks will adjust to any changing circumstances.

It is also the case that commercial banks would have various policy options to offset any likely practical effects of the CBDC on the volume of their deposits. Various mitigating options were suggested by witnesses who gave evidence to the Committee. For instance, it would be possible for the banks to shift the balance of their funding towards a higher proportion of wholesale deposit funding. Such a move may require increased liquidity and some tightening of credit criteria, although estimating the magnitude of this potentially negative impact will be difficult. An alternative would be to seek higher quality collateral against loans.

It would also be possible to limit the amount of CBDC held by customers. The Committee –despite oral evidence from Eswar Passad (Passad 2021) that the Bahamas had capped the CBDC household customer holdings, with higher amounts for business accounts – suggested that such a rule might disincentivize CBDC holdings. Were interest to be paid on holdings, this could be tiered to manage investment behaviour rather than impose strict limits.

A related issue is the high level of disintermediation that could occur during a future financial crisis, such as a bank run. This eventuality could be ameliorated for most customers by deposit insurance, introduced after the global financial crisis, or higher levels of tiered equity held by banks under international regulations, or by other protective actions of the central bank.

The level of disintermediation is also extremely sensitive to CBDC design choices, as the report acknowledges (see Chapter 2). The BIS has suggested that there may be firmer evidence from the piloting of retail CBDCs in China and the Bahamas. However, these two examples are not necessarily representative of the majority of jurisdictions and monetary systems and sit at the opposite ends of the spectrum in terms of the motivation for launching CBDCs. The issue was, perhaps, best summed up from the commercial banks' perspective, albeit pessimistically, by Patrick Donohan of Barclays, in his evidence to the Lords' enquiry: "the decision over whether the Bank of England should implement CBDC thus presents a trade-off: a doubtful improvement in payments efficiency at the cost of potentially more expensive retail borrowing" (Donohan 2021).

Without sufficiently firm evidence to determine the level of disintermediation, the Lords report's belief that the level could be high enough (even higher than the BoE's illustrative example of 20 per cent) to act as a significant deterrent to a central bank from introducing a retail CBDC, appears speculative and unnecessarily negative. Contingency planning would clearly be required for bank run scenarios. Before placing too much weight on the uncertain potential level of disintermediation in judging the value of CBDCs, the following Lords' report recommendation seems apposite, "We recommend that the Bank of England conduct further studies to assess what would be the effect on the banking system if more than 20 per cent of deposits converted to CBDC".

The BoE produced a consultation document on CBDCs in 2021 (Bank of England 2021c). It published the responses on 22 March 2022 and is continuing further detailed examination of the approach it might take in moving forward in pursuing any future implementation of any of the design models of a retail CBDC.

Customer access

The issue of privacy is one of the most important considerations for consumers when questioned about CBDCs. The problem is more complex than it at first appears. Trust is rarely raised as a problem in customer dealings with commercial banks, probably because of long-standing familiarity between the parties.

There are two categories of privacy: identity privacy, intended to preserve the identities of both the sender and recipient of a transaction, and the time of the transaction. Second, is transaction privacy, intended to preserve the anonymity of the nature of the transaction (Brookings 2021). It may be that maintaining identity privacy where commercial banks have a key operational role in managing transactions is less important than sometimes acknowledged, as indicated above, familiarity breeds trust. However, it will be important more generally to protect transaction networks from revealing the timing of all transactions by cryptographic means, such as constant-time algorithms. The issue here *is transaction privacy.*

An alternative approach has been suggested by the Bank of England (Bank of England 2020). The BoE proposes to establish, via an API, a payment interface provider (PIP) who would be responsible for providing only pseudonymous identity information on the transactions to the central bank, with only the PIP recording the associated personal identity information. The PIP could then be requested by an authorized investigator to provide information on accounts suspected of avoiding regulatory compliance with AML or other criminal activity. It is not clear that this system fully safeguards identity or transaction privacy as it relies on the PIP otherwise protecting the identity information. Insofar as commercial banks would be concerned then the relaxed view apparently taken by customers of privacy protection, may well apply. However, this may not be the case with other newer payment providers, who *may* become holders and transactors of CBDCs.

However, another challenge to *identity privacy* protection is the need to support mechanisms to enforce regulatory and compliance rules, as states want to detect and prevent criminal activities, such as international rules covering AML, and to ensure financial stability. Some form of oversight and surveillance of transactions will be required by the relevant public authorities. Some may argue that potentially this could provide governments with information to track citizens. This fear may be exaggerated and even in China, where higher levels of individual surveillance *may* be suspected, e-CNY transactions below a certain level do not require the divulgence of personal identity information. In practice, CBDC transactions will be operated so that significant identity privacy protection is afforded to customers while permitting, as currently, some measure of visibility for authorized law enforcement agencies.

There are obviously jurisdictional cultural values in operation when assessing the needs for identity privacy among the civil populations involved. This also flags the difference between the complete anonymity and multiusage of physical cash, as opposed to CBDCs and, for that matter credit cards. It also strengthens the arguments for the retention of cash, notwithstanding its declining use in some jurisdictions.

As far as transaction privacy is concerned, the amount that a user is sending can be hidden using encryption. It is equally important that users cannot send more money than they actually possess. Hence there is a novel requirement, specifically in the case of the central bank CBDC digital *retail* money, for cryptographic means (see Chapter 3) to prove that the amount being sent does not exceed the current balance available, but without revealing the amount of that balance.

Privacy cannot be implemented without consideration of accessibility to, and verifiability of, the CBDC digital currency holder and transactors. This suggests that eliciting the concerns of the general public about CBDCs (including privacy issue) requires careful explanation and consideration by the public before any decision on implementation is made.

Many of the issues raised in relation to personal customers in an era of CBDCs are also applicable to *corporate* clients, especially SMEs, where there is frequently a coincidence between the personal bank of the owner-manager/ director of the company and the company account (Lloyd 2021). However, for larger corporates, CBDC offers other possibilities that require extra consideration. First is that of surveillance, which aims to prevent money laundering. AML compliance, because of the current embedded nature of the regulatory infrastructure relating to anti-money laundering and know your customer processes of banks, is able to check false reporting. The advent of CBDCS and distributed ledger/blockchain technology is likely to automate this process further but will require sophisticated algorithms to avoid any increase in false notifications.

Linked to the above concern is the need for a wider appreciation among central banks about the interface between new commercial bank digital technology platform systems and the development of corporate programmable distributed ledger systems that automate supply-chain payments and other business interactions within those supply chains. The main issues surrounding CBDC programmability (Sandner *et al.* 2020), smart contracts, and related database technology, were detailed in Chapter 3. The issue for CBDC technology interactions between corporations and commercial banks is the need to take account of the future need for links between CBDC payments smart contract programmability and the Internet of Things.

The role of credit card providers

The Bahamian retail CBDC project involves MasterCard (see the Appendices). The credit card company is interested in working with the Bahamas Central Bank to deliver CBDC payment services to unbanked individuals on remote islands, who have limited access to cash. Visa (Visa 2022) is also becoming involved more widely with retail CBDCs, linking with ConsenSys and their Quorum database platform. Their involvement, as with MasterCard, is to provide a user-friendly interface for the consumer wishing to use the digital money provided by the CBDC for daily spending. As Catherine Gu, Visa's Head of CBDC explains:

> We (Visa) envision a user experience that looks very familiar to how you pay today. If CBDC networks are seamlessly integrated into your existing banking app, you'd be able to use your CBDC-linked Visa card at the checkout. Or tap your digital wallet – loaded with your CBDC funds and payment credential – to pay securely at any of the 80 million merchant locations worldwide that accept Visa and any of its connected networks, all through existing retailers' existing payment terminal. It's a familiar experience for people around the world. (Visa 2022, no page)

Obviously, Visa and MasterCard are competitors, although their approach – aside from the choices of distributed database technology provider (and there may be more than one) – will be similar in terms of the product offering.

The main reason for Mastercard's involvement in the Bahamas retail CBDC project was the wide ownership and use of smart phones across that islands' community. Visa has a similar interest, given that approximately two-thirds of the world's unbanked population own a mobile phone. The distribution of CBDCs via smart phones that can readily be linked to mobile physical cards, enable people living in remote areas, such as island communities, and in many African and Asian countries to be reached.

The marketing aim of the credit card companies appears to be to (1) provide an alternative hardware device storage for CBDCs, separate from smartphones, for those not wishing to use smartphones, and (2) somehow tie the use of the smartphone CBDC user to merchants registered with the credit cards. It is not clear how this second route can be secured. Moreover, there is also the issue of charges levied on the merchants, currently around 4 per cent of the transaction value.

Presumably the intention is to have retail CBDCs (if and when launched) accepted by businesses and retailers, via connection to the existing payment infrastructure through an API layer on top of CBDC platform networks. The credit card companies expect that central banks will wish to integrate any delivery of digital money to the general public together with the resource support, expertise and involvement of the private sector, including credit card companies.

In technology terms it will be necessary for the main distributed ledger databases (ConsenSys Quorum in the case of Visa) to be registered as complying with common standards and, crucially, to demonstrate interoperability between public and private networks. Currently, there is no published international compliance standard available, though there is an ISO Technical Committee ISO/ TC 307 and an information standard ISO 22739:2020. Use-cases are being deployed to test both the interoperability of the DLT and the linking of credit card companies' payments modules to the CBDC issuance databases. The Quant Overledger interoperable gateway is an example (see Chapter 3).

Interestingly, given the concerns about using CBDC issuance as an opportunity for monetary policy and fiscal policy innovation, Visa suggest that one potential use-case could be to explore the potential for sending "fast payments to a targeted set of users and programme specific spending parameters", which would require further investigation.

Other monetary system reform options

It has been suggested, by a number of US commentators, and latterly by the UK House of Lords, that the failures of the current payments systems, central banks and of commercial banks could be resolved by reforms other than by the introduction of CBDCs. It could be argued that the two initiatives by the Bank of England – the Omnibus account and the RTGS Renewal Programme – are examples of this.

The aim of the BoE's Omnibus account, according to the Bank, is to enable RTGS to interface with a wider range of payment systems, including those using DLT:

> Under the new model, an operator of a payment system can hold funds in the omnibus account to fund their participants' balances with central bank money. This will allow them to offer innovative payment services, while having the security of central bank money settlement. They can support a wide range of high-value payments, which could range from a commercial bank buying government bonds to a small business paying their suppliers. (Bank of England 2021b, no page)

The RTGS Renewal Programme has the wider objective of developing an enhanced RTGS service, anticipating future demands, increasing user access, functionality and resilience, and providing interoperability with outside payment systems (Bank of England 2021e). The new system will be fully operational in the spring of 2024, to enable fast clearance of payments, such as high-value payments in house purchasing. There will be little impact on end-users, but the internal processes will be more efficient and future-proofed in terms of new standards (ISO 20022) and potential use of new technology (DLT). Although this is a welcome initiative, replicated in the US and in some other jurisdictions, such as the eurozone, it is not clear that it is sufficient to negate the overall benefits of CBDCs that are not simply restricted to faster payments.

Others have also suggested that the balance of costs and benefits appears too narrow to justify using CBDCs to resolve relatively minor problems with the current monetary system that could be fixed in other ways without the attendant risks of introducing CBDCs. Aside from the UK House of Lords, representatives of this view are Cecchetti and Schoenholtz (2021), who suggest that in most advanced economies digital money is already used for payment transactions, via privately-run payment networks, through the digital liabilities (money) of private commercial banks, and they question the need for central banks to issue retail digital currencies. They suggest that improving payment systems, dealing with threats from stablecoins, evasion of AML, and the effectiveness of monetary policy are possible *without* CBDCs. However, the remedial suggestions of Ceccetti and Schoenholtz are less than convincing, even if the points they raise need addressing.

Assessment of relative impacts

In all four of the monetary architecture design options outlined in Chapters 2 and 3 (direct-citizen interface, hybrid account/token-based, intermediated account based and indirect provision), the retail CBDC is issued by the central bank alone. Three allow for either account or token-based delivery and access, the exception being the intermediated model that appears to be predicated for use as an account-based model.

In the direct CBDC model the central bank handles all payments in real time and thus keeps a record of all retail holdings. Should this model be preferred then the outcome would find the central bank effectively competing for deposits with commercial banks. This competition for deposits, especially if the central bank were to offer attractive relative interest rates would then be likely to encourage significant disintermediation, and at times of financial crisis may trigger an undesirable bank run. Despite the attraction of simplicity, this design is unlikely to be adopted in the majority of modern developed countries. In these countries the model, assuming even a modest take-up by the public, would involve novel and considerable extra work by central banks, including processing retail management of accounts or tokens, in addition to the traditional, key role of the central bank. It is also unclear how receptive to the issuance and receipt of digital money direct from the central bank the general public would be. In developing countries with a high proportion of scattered, isolated, and unbanked populations with limited access to cash, the model has its attractions, as in The Bahamas and the East Caribbean for instance.

The hybrid model would, as now, involve the commercial banks/payment service provider handling the retail, real-time financial payment transactions, removing that burden from central banks. However, the central bank will still need to record and retain a copy of all retail CBDC holdings. This would be necessary also in the event of a technical or other failure of one payment service provider, enabling transfer to another. In this model the customer/client holding the digital money, retains a direct claim on the central bank in the event of loss or dispute. This hybrid model, adopted by China's PBOC, could be viewed as a transitional design for modern, developed countries, as it is not clear whether it will be the final resting place for China. The decision whether to adopt this model as a permanent design may depend on the cultural values of the country concerned and hence degree of centralized control over the monetary system in the country. This control may be linked to the desire for government surveillance of citizens. However, it is noticeable in China that below a certain value of the transaction there is no need for direct monitoring by the PBOC. Direct government monitoring by the state of all citizens at all times in any sizeable country is in any case an impossible task.

The intermediated account-based design is similar to the hybrid model, with the key difference being that the central bank maintains a central ledger of corresponding wholesale transactions, matching the retail activity. Again, there is a direct CBDC claim on the central bank. In this model, the commercial bank may be said to be acting as a *custodian* of the customer/client digital money. The central bank will require to maintain a record of *only* wholesale payments, via regular notification of the matched retail payment transactions. This is the same as it is now with the current monetary systems and the correlation between the commercial bank private digital money net retail transactions and the central bank wholesale final clearance and settlement.

From the position of the commercial bank/payment service provider this model is very similar to the current system. The only difference is the need for specific prudential and privacy safeguards on the CBDC accounts. Hence, this may be preferred by the commercial banks only insofar as this model is account-based, as opposed to the hybrid design which could also be tokenized. From the central bank perspective, the benefit of this design is that it is relieved of the responsibility of not only having to manage retail transactions, but also to avoid the necessity of having to record and retain retail transactions. This model design may be selected by a number of countries, though as has been suggested, the indirect model involves the least disruption of all to the monetary architecture than any of the other three models.

In the indirect CBDC architecture design, users of the CBDC, unlike in all other models do not have a direct claim on the central bank. Instead, the CBDC is issued to the commercial banks/payment service providers. Customers may then set up CBDC accounts or they can request the issuance as tokens directly attributed to them via a cryptographic key. However, the commercial bank is unlikely to grant such a request, and the customer is unlikely to request the digital money in the form of tokens. Again, the central bank is only required to update the wholesale accounts. From the perspective of the commercial banks/payment service providers this model has effectively the same operational architecture as the commercial bank–central bank structure familiar to customers at present. Notwithstanding the fact that the commercial banks will be liable for any claim from the customer, as the central bank is not directly involved, it is possible it will be an acceptable model for them, and possibly for their customers. From a central bank perspective this design involves the least possible change, and hence disruption, to the current, established monetary system. This may turn out to be the preferred model for the majority of central banks, either as a transitional model or, possibly, a permanent model for some.

More generally, as far as CBDCs are concerned, their deployment – set in the context of the era of increasing socio-economic digitization – could be viewed as an opportunity to address problems with existing payments systems and the challenges in the monetary arena posed by private alternative finance platforms, including stablecoins, to the key stabilizing and trust roles played by central banks in issuing fiat currencies. The issue is whether there is an overall net benefit. This net benefit may be judged by the benefits of increased efficiency and lower costs against possible concerns about data governance and perhaps wider concerns about future uses of retail CBDCs. Viewed in this light, retail CBDCs could lead to payment methods that, for instance, obviate the problem of the high merchant costs (not seen by their users) of credit and debit cards, despite technological progress potentially lowering costs.

Given the potential for instability created by unregulated issuers of stablecoins, Chapter 2 suggested that CBDCs also represent a means for central banks to maintain the public trust-anchor in the new digital age, meeting the potential challenge from private (currently unregulated) stablecoins and the creation of private monetary silos. Some private, corporate and even banking interests in the US, while not appearing to disagree with the argument that a fiat currency, supported by the role of the central bank, is a public good (compensating for negative network effects in the financial system), are not currently supportive of this position. Of course, should regulation of stablecoin issuers involve the same level and nature of regulation and prudential safeguards as applied to commercial banks then such an outcome would increase the competition for the current commercial bank incumbents. The current banks might grumble, but this outcome would likely be in the public interest. It is not clear that such an outcome is desired by some of the private stablecoin issuers. The disagreements about the type of regulation in the US appear to be as much ideological as technical.

The focus of central banks, and the BIS, on *wholesale* CBDCs (wCBDCs) in the context of cross-border financial transfers appears appropriate and timely. The threats to financial stability, from stablecoins are more serious at a global level than at a domestic one. The international cooperation, involving the BIS hub, China, and other countries' central and commercial banks on various projects to conceptualize, test and pilot innovative structural approaches using fiat currencies, has yielded promising results in terms of lowered costs and increased speeds of transmission, with enhanced security and resilience.

The use of forms of distributed ledgers, smart contracts and tokens representing currencies and other assets, such as bonds, has demonstrated a strong potential for utilizing wCBDCs within validated legal constraints (Helvetia Project 2022). Given the level of progress achieved it seems likely that over the next few years there will be a regional implementation of this approach. With the progressive development of private, corporate stablecoin cross-border financial transfers, the apparent degree of urgency, being demonstrated by the BIS to establish an internationally acceptable prototype system, appears justified. From a commercial bank perspective, this initiative does not threaten their role within the monetary system, indeed it will enhance it. The advent of wCBDCs in facilitating fiat currency, denominated assets across jurisdictional borders will also provide experience in collaboration with central banks in using innovative DLT and smart contracts. This experience will be valuable in the event that retail CBDCs are introduced.

Conclusion

The impacts on commercial banks of CBDC issuance will vary, as will the potential responses of the various banks, faced with the range of choices for introducing CBDCs. There will also be cultural behaviour factors (on privacy for instance) across monetary jurisdictions. The close involvement of commercial banks with the central bank in discussing the implications for their banking operations and structure is imperative. Insofar as the use of deposit accounts may be significantly threatened, as a result of retail CBDCs, disintermediation is a specific area where banks will need to be prepared to react. However, the likely impact of disintermediation is difficult to estimate, with a barely useful range of impact between 4 per cent and 52 per cent suggested. The actual impacts will depend on the CBDC models used, the reactions of customers/clients, and the reaction of the commercial banks.

It will be important for the central banks to carefully analyse, before any introduction of CBDCs, the various impacts on commercial banks and the efficient working of the monetary system, and more widely on any damaging influence on their economies arising from impacts on maturity transformation and any associated problems of liquidity provision. The impacts on commercial banks and their intermediation role will thus depend critically on the design of the retail CBDC. More generally, the commercial banks need, in any event, to plan for a more uncertain future, dominated by increasing innovation in digitization.

It seems likely that central banks will be cautious in the model they choose for launching retail CBDCs, probably selecting an accounts-based approach, using either the indirect or the intermediation model design. These selections have two benefits: first, avoiding the central bank having to adopt either a burdensome technological operational workload or the operational service provision of the commercial banks, its role would be restricted to CBDC issuance and monitoring. Second, to avoid significant divergence on the part of commercial banks' customers/clients from their existing, and familiar, monetary behaviour. It is extremely unlikely that central banks in any large, developed jurisdiction will wish to offer credit directly to either businesses or citizens.

The anticipated impact of CBDCs on commercial banks appears to be manageable, providing the banks recognize the importance of responding to the rapidly innovating digital environment. Nowhere is this more noticeable than in the arena of cross-border financial transfers. Many central banks are involving themselves in projects developing, integrating and extending their RTGS systems, via distributed ledger systems, smart contracts and cryptography within the new fiat currency architectures to improve financial transfers. There is little to worry commercial banks about this area of development, and commercial banks are indeed participating and gathering expertise themselves within several wholesale CBDC projects.

5
THE REGIONAL AND INTERNATIONAL NEXUS

The development of stablecoins and their use in cross-border financial transfers has the potential to pose a threat to global financial stability. The global financial system is inherently unstable, reflecting the increasing dysfunction of the Bretton Woods global trade and finance settlement that was based on the US dollar as the principal global medium of exchange, store of value and unit of account. The deterioration in the effectiveness of this global system is being accelerated by the shift in global trade, consumption and economic growth towards the Asia-Pacific supra-region accompanied by the growing inadequacy of stable global financial reserves (SDRs) owned and managed by the IMF.

It seems likely that, unless central banks collaborate internationally in opening up the possibilities for the introduction of retail and wholesale CBDCs, then unintended negative consequences may occur. For example, if Sweden – the "first mover" among EU countries (albeit they may not now be the first to issue a CBDC) – introduced a digital krona, then its use could leak across Nordic countries. China has already suggested that their e-CNY might be used for regional trade transactions between China, Japan, South Korea and Hong Kong. The advent of China's exploration of cross-border retail and wholesale CBDCs has been linked to concern about the potential of extension of e-CNY for wider international payments. Some US commentators have expressed fears of its challenge to the dollar as a reserve currency. The Bank of International Settlements is considering all these issues. The significant emphasis placed on the use of CBDCs by the BIS in relation to cross-border payments related to trade, tourism and capital movements is indicative of the concern exhibited by central banks about the use of unregulated stablecoins for international payments. The various central bank CBDC activities could be regarded as a precursor to the eventual adoption of a global reserve digital currency. A move the US will be likely to strongly resist, despite the use of the dollar as the main reserve currency being a mixed blessing, as Barry Eichengreen (2017) and other economists have pointed out. This explains some of the resistance to CBDCs among US financial institutions and economists.

The new global political economy

The global axis of GDP, consumption and trade is shifting rapidly towards the Asia-Pacific region. Asia's share of global trade in goods rose from 28 per cent in 2000–02 to 33 per cent in 2015–17; its share of consumption rising similarly from 23 per cent of the global total to 28 per cent in the same period. In purchasing power parity terms Asia's share of global GDP rose from 32 per cent in 2000 to 42 per cent in 2017 and is projected to rise to around 52 per cent by 2040. Europe's share fell from 26 per cent to 22 per cent and the North America share from 25 per cent to 18 per cent over the 2000 to 2017 period. Since 2002 Asia's share of global capital flows has increased from 13 per cent to 23 per cent (Tonby *et al.* 2019).

However, these trends have been accompanied by a marked shift to intra-regional integration, not only in goods but also in cross-border services trade and in terms of greater financial integration. This shift is noted by Oliver Tonby *et al.* (2019):

> Asia is not only rising in scale but is also integrating rapidly, arguably setting the pace for a new stage of globalization: regionalization. Globally observed shifts toward less trade-intensive goods-producing value chains, and cross-border services trade happening faster than goods trade, for instance, are more obvious in Asia than elsewhere. Asia's trade intensity dropped from 20 to 14 percent between 2007 and 2017. On all eight dimensions studied, Asia's integration is increasing and there is an observable shift toward regionalization. For instance, 60 percent of goods traded by Asian economies are within the region, 71 percent of Asian investment in start-ups and 59 percent of foreign direct investment (FDI) is intraregional, and 74 percent of Asian travellers travel within the region.

The significant and rapid development of regional institutions and collaborations, not least with respect to central banks, is supporting this process. Inevitably these trends are accompanied by financial innovation in payment and wider monetary integration, to facilitate this global and regional concentration of economic growth, consumption and trade. Some of the motivation has also come from the desire to move away from financial systems dominated by the US dollar. Moreover, it is the Asian countries that are initiating the development of international standards in the database technologies involved (ACM 2021). An indication of China's role in the setting of international standards is the POBC Digital Currency Research Institute (DCRI) (Lloyd & Savic 2021). In July 2020, at a plenary meeting of the Telecommunication Union Standardization Sector

(ITU-T) Study Group (SG 16), the DCRI led a proposal to establish a Financial Distribution Ledger Application Guide as an international standard. The guide provides a framework, within which any country can carry out the planning and layout of financial blockchain international standard systems, adding sub-standards, such as reference architecture, risk control, security and privacy protection, and financial blockchain business specifications in various fields.

This initiative has also enabled China to establish the Blockchain Service Network (BSN), that will also, initially in Asia, support the adoption of the e-CNY. In September 2021, BSN started operating in South Korea (Ledger Insights 2021), as the report of the deal, led by Red Date Technology Company indicates:

> BSN was founded by the Chinese government's State Information Center (SIC) along with Red Date, China Mobile and China UnionPay. The Chinese network supports only enterprise blockchain technologies but makes them publicly accessible, whereas the international network additionally supports numerous public blockchains such as Ethereum, EOS, Polkadot, NEO and Tezos. A key focus is to try to create interoperability between different blockchain offerings.
>
> (Ledger Insights 2021, no page)

In China itself, the BSN has expanded to over 100 nodes in 80 cities, where it provides infrastructure for smart city technologies. It has also been installed in at least eight cities outside China, and has attracted cooperation from Google, Microsoft and Amazon web services, although most of the BSN infrastructure is hosted on China-based cloud providers. The network is also integrated with some of the largest public blockchain networks, including Ethereum, EOS, Tezos, Hyperledger and ConsenSys Quorum. The long-term intention is for BSN to get blockchains to communicate, in the same manner that computer networks interact, using the internet protocol.

Accompanying and utilizing this initiative, the digitization of the yuan does mean that a blockchain network across its Asian trading partners and along the Belt and Road Initiative (BRI), and its parallel initiative the Digital Silk Road, could enable the widespread use of the e-CNY for transactions (Lloyd & Savic 2021). This would still be a major step-up for China in the world's financial system. The US is concerned about this development. Robert Murray of the influential US think tank, the Foreign Policy Research Institute:

> The BSN will, in part, support the global adoption and distribution of the digital yuan, and together, they could centralize financial network infrastructures within China's technological ecosystem. U.S. soft

power has long benefitted from its dominance of the world's financial and technological infrastructure, and a successful BSN could threaten U.S. dominance in these areas ... If successful over the long term, the digital yuan could threaten the economic and strategic interests of the United States ... The digital yuan is positioned to serve as the lifeblood of Beijing's international economic agenda, which is underpinned by the expansion of a China-centric digital ecosystem that encompasses game-changing technology such as 5G, Industry 4.0, economic and social surveillance, global satellite navigation, and autonomous machine-to-machine communications and payments. The perniciousness of the digital yuan is the speed and stickiness with which it will enable Beijing to lock in gains in international economic influence with those that adopt it ... A digital yuan in global circulation and a China-dominated blockchain infrastructure would go a long way toward cementing Beijing's economic influence and soft power around the world.

(Murray 2021, no page)

The concept of a global reserve currency and global unit of account has a long history dating from the Bretton Woods conference in 1944. The Bretton Woods settlement instituted a dollar-gold standard, with a system of fixed exchange rates, which lasted until the early 1970s, when the US abandoned the link with gold and the now familiar dollar-standard took its place, together with "fixed but flexible" exchange rates. The dollar is the world's principal reserve currency, the global medium of exchange, store of value, and unit of account for international trade purposes. In the 2000s the euro challenged the dollar as a medium of exchange, but in the other two roles the dollar remains dominant. Despite China's strength in trade, it has only a miniscule role – less than 3 per cent – as a global medium of exchange.

The global financial system is reliant on not only international SDR reserves held by the IMF, but more substantially on "currency swaps" between central banks and, increasingly since the global financial crisis, a variety of regional financial arrangements (RFAs) (IMF 2021: 2). The IMF reports an increase reflecting the expansion of the bilateral swap arrangements during the global financial crisis and during the recent Covid-19 pandemic, as well as the establishment of new regional financial arrangements, especially in Europe (such as the European Stability Mechanism) and in South-East Asia (the Chiang Mai Initiative Multilateralization). The IMF had also more than doubled its available resources in the aftermath of the global financial crisis. The increased bilateral swap arrangements, primarily the US Federal Reserve swaps, provided prompt liquidity support, helping to stabilize the global financial markets and capital flows to emerging market economies. The substantial increases in regional reserves and the proportion of total global reserves represented by IMF SDRs, falling from 90 per cent to 25 per cent, is a significant indicator of future trends. Nonetheless, changes in the regional dimension of global finance have been developing for some time and there has been a surge in regional reserves funding since 2010 (Rhee *et al.* 2013).

After the global financial crisis, the major bilateral swap lines (BSLs) were led by the US Federal Reserve, together with five other central banks that form the so-called "C6 swap network": the ECB, the Bank of England, the Bank of Japan, the Bank of Canada and the Swiss National Bank (Mehrling 2015). Interestingly, as an indicator of the chronic instability of the current global exchange rate system, the Federal Reserve renewed the temporary Bilateral Swap Lines (BSLs) with the five major central banks and converted them into permanent and unlimited standing facilities in 2013. The C6 swap network represents the ultimate line of defence against new systemic financial crises in the Offshore US-Dollar System. The C6, led by the Fed, thus form a multilateral forum which acts as an "international lender of last resort". As long as the Fed is willing to support the mechanism, it continues to protect the western markets, but it may not afford much protection for emerging markets across the world. A large swathe of the world's countries is likely to seek support from China, ASEAN and the BRICS.

A recent IMF study (Perks *et al.* 2021) argues that although BSLs can be an important source of liquidity support, in some cases they might contribute to the prolongation of weak policies. Its empirical analysis provides little evidence that BSLs promote sound policies following their extension, which may not be surprising given that BSLs do not usually attach policy conditionality. The IMF proposes that BSLs should be accompanied by an IMF-supported programme to help the recipient country address its balance of payments needs and to strengthen the effectiveness of the global financial safety net.

The increase in regional financial currency reserves points not only to chronic global financial instability, but also to the further diversification of the global economy and global reserves, with a strong Asia-Pacific regional dimension. The Chiang Mai Initiative on Multilateralization (Khor 2017), for example, is the multilateral currency swap arrangement between ASEAN+3 members. Coming into effect in March 2010 its core objectives are to address balance-of-payment and short-term liquidity difficulties in the region and to supplement existing international financial arrangements. The contracting parties to the CMIM Agreement consist of the finance ministries and central banks of Brunei Darussalam, Cambodia, China, Indonesia, Japan, South Korea, Lao PDR, Malaysia, Myanmar, Philippines, Singapore, Thailand, Vietnam and the Hong Kong Monetary Authority. In 2014 the facility stood at US$240 billion and in March 2021 (PBOC 2021a) the IMF de-linked portion of the facility was raised from 30 per cent to 40 per cent. This facility is supported by a separate

ASEAN swap arrangement of US$330 billion and is able to tap into the US$6.9 trillion foreign exchange reserves of the CMIM members.

However, this move away from a US-dominated global financial and monetary system is not confined to the Asia-Pacific region. There has been the development of new institutions linked to the BRICS, such as the New Development Bank (NDB) and the BRICS Contingent Reserve Arrangement (CRA). These institutions were built by Brazil, Russia, India, China and South Africa because of concerns about the effective control of the global monetary system by the US and its dollar dominance. There is particular concern about the World Bank and the International Monetary Fund (IMF), where distrust of the IMF's solutions and conditionalities are high, given the bitter experience of the IMF adjustment programme throughout much of the Global South. These new institutions have been slow to develop since their establishment at the beginning of the twenty-first century, but since 2020 they have become more active.

These shifts in the global economy arguably suggest the need for a new global financial and exchange rate settlement. The establishment and wider deployment of the e-CNY emphasizes the regional development potential of the new cross-border multicurrency CBDC architecture being piloted by central banks. Although not directly connected, these developments may act as a further spur to a radical rethinking of the global trade and exchange-rate system.

Notwithstanding the above, the US dollar continues to be the global reserve currency, representing 60 per cent of the total in 2021, although it is subject to a slow decline (Arslanalp *et al* 2022). The next largest currency is the euro at around 20 per cent. The yuan is less than 3 per cent. However, as indicated above, it is certainly possible that the share of the e-CNY use in transactions will rise substantially as a medium of exchange, to reflect the trade strength of China, its Asian regional dominance, and its projected use of blockchain technology. Whether the e-CNY increases its share as a store of value will depend on how far China is willing to go in terms of its stated goal of full liberalization of capital flows. It seems likely that for some time China will want to keep a significant measure of control over capital movements in and out of China. The dollar will remain the global unit of account.

There is little sign that the growth of trade, investment and consumption in the Asia-Pacific region is likely to falter over the coming decades. Indeed, western countries are still targeting exports on the region, despite the region's production and consumption of its own services increasing. Hence, whereas it might be thought that western countries may have a comparative advantage this is no longer necessarily the case. The technological strength of several Asia-Pacific countries militates against success in services exports from the West.

Russia's invasion of Ukraine in February 2022 introduced further global instability with western nations imposing significant trade and monetary sanctions on Russia. In addition to creating short-term damage to the Russian economy, there has also been consequences for energy supplies and rising domestic costs in the West. The sanctions are intended to isolate the Russian economy from global trade and the global monetary system. China, having been unwilling to support the sanctions against Russia, is being caught up in these wider monetary sanctions. Neither the short-term nor the long-term consequences of this US-led use of economic sanctions appears to have been explored by the politicians taking these major decisions that have global implications (see a detailed Chinese perspective on a speech by Anthony Blinken, US Secretary of State from the Chinese Ministry of Foreign Affairs (MFA 2022)). Whether depriving Russia of access to the SWIFT international payments inter-bank system, effectively run by the US, will have an impact on the outcome of the war is unclear, whether it will have a lasting effect on the global trends and developments in the global financial system is even less certain.

China

China's interest in extending the use of its e-CNY outside of China appeared initially to be restricted to its narrow, albeit significant, Asian regional trade use. The original idea for the digital yuan came from ten members of the Chinese People's Political Consultative Conference (CPPCC) (Lloyd & Savic 2021). The stated aim was for the digital currency to be used as a cross-border payments network, supporting a free trade agreement between China, Japan, South Korea and Hong Kong, backed by a basket of the four currencies. The ratios of these in the "official stablecoin" would be determined by the economic weight of the associated economies. This proposal has been subsequently overtaken by events and China's involvement in an international approach led by the BIS to cross-border wCBDC.

Nonetheless, beyond China's immediate regional trade borders, as suggested above, the e-CNY could help facilitate the internationalization of the yuan as a medium of exchange. According to the Society for Worldwide Interbank Financial Telecommunication (SWIFT), the world's largest international electronic payment system, the renminbi was only used in 1.9 per cent of all international payments in July 2020. By comparison, the US dollar and the euro were used in 38.8 per cent and 36.5 per cent of transactions respectively. A joint venture involving the PBOC, CIPS and SWIFT was set up at the beginning of 2021 (Reuters 2021). The present Chinese International Payment System (CIPS) runs over the SWIFT network.

Payment systems are closely related to trade. In the context of the development and use of CBDCs for cross-border payments the implementation of a wider use of the e-CNY for trade within a multicountry currency area (not necessarily a formal currency union) would be an advantage to China if use of the renmimbi increased. Such a development would then be comparable with the wide use of the US dollar and the euro, well beyond their strict monetary jurisdictions.

The suggestion by China for a free trade area covering Japan, South Korea and Hong Kong, if accepted, would then mean that China's digital currency, backed by an appropriately weighted basket of currencies, would become the regional payments currency across that free trade zone. It is not yet clear how such an initiative would fit with other currency union suggestions made over the past decade within areas covered by ASEAN+3 (Randhawa 2020). These developments are also linked to the recently initiated, January 2022, RECEP trade agreement.

However, the US barring of dollar-based transactions as a sanction against Russia, and in light of other US financial sanctions against China, the Chinese are rushing to build a payment network independent of the dollar. Given China's increasing dominance in regional and international trade, it is clearly motivated to take defensive action and build its own currency for trade.

The speed of development and piloting of the e-CNY is evidence of China's desire to avoid too great a dependence on the US dollar. Given the extent of its trading relationships, particularly its Asia-Pacific regional dominance and its strong trading and investment positions in both Africa and the Middle East, the use of the e-CNY in these geographical areas is a practical solution. The exchange rates of several East Asian countries already informally track the yuan, itself partially linked to the value of the US dollar, although it is not clear how long this "crawling peg" arrangement will last.

China's drive to increase the international use of its currency predates the e-CNY. In 2021, a Forkast video report on China Blockchain (Forkast 2021) commented that:

> In December 2019, to facilitate a US$54billion China–Pakistan Economic Corridor (PEACE) project [see Lloyd & Savic 2021], Pakistan announced the yuan as its second national currency – a role long occupied by the dollar. Six months later, Turkey Telekom agreed to use the yuan for import payments. ... Between 2000 and 2015, China's trade settlement in yuan increased from roughly zero to US$1.1 trillion, according to the National Bureau of Asian Research, close to a third of the country's external trade. But even by 2021, only 2.5 per cent of international payments worldwide were transacted in yuan, according to the CSIS China Project, compared to 39 per cent in the US dollar and 36 per cent in the euro. (Forkast 2021, no page)

The apparent low usage of the yuan in these figures, derived from the SWIFT messaging service may understate the use of the yuan in cross-border settlement, in relation to China's external trade. The PBOC 2021 Annual Report on the Renminbi) Internationalization reported that:

> In 2020, the cross-border RMB settlement grew by 44 per cent on a yearly basis, accounting for 46 per cent of the total cross-border settlement in RMB and foreign currencies in China. The attractiveness of RMB assets for foreign investors has been further boosted, with the amount of domestic RMB-denominated financial assets held by foreign entities growing quickly. The new type of mutually beneficial partnership based on RMB usage has become more robust.   (PBOC 2021c)

Since 2006, China has been reducing its dependence on international trade (Lloyd & Savic 2021), as a percentage of GDP it fell from 65 per cent in 2006 to 37 per cent in 2021 (World Bank 2021). However, the Chinese currency is only used for trade transaction purposes in less than 2–3 per cent of those transactions. Reluctance to use the renminbi is partly to do with the general geopolitical antagonisms towards China, promoted by the US, and partly due to the perception of China as a dominant trade partner.

China has recently, introduced an "offshore renminbi" (CNH) subject to free market valuation, with Hong Kong as the global hub for CNH clearing and trading. However, the CNH project's wider circulation of the e-CNY across Asia-Pacific, plus its use along the BRI, offers a far higher likelihood of expanding the e-CNY as an international medium of exchange. This action has been accompanied by other initiatives that include: regional currency swap agreements with 36 countries, providing necessary liquidity when required; inclusion of the renminbi in the IMF's special drawing rights (SDR) basket; creation of free trade zones in Shanghai and the provinces of Guangdong, Tianjin and Fujian; gradual liberalization of capital controls, especially on foreign direct investment, and the alignment of national legislation with international legal standards; and, finally, issuing the off-shore purchase of so-called "dim sum" bonds, allowing foreign investors to acquire directly renminbi-denominated assets (Lloyd & Savic 2021: 137–8).

The overall longer-term international monetary policy aim of China was articulated in 2009, by the then-Governor of the PBOC (Zhou 2009), who suggested the need for an "international reserve currency" to "secure global financial stability". The close involvement of the PBOC in the BIS managed m-CBDC Bridge project suggests that this long-term objective remains, in which the development of regional wholesale CBDC cross-border systems could provide a long-term, evolutionary path to a global digital currency.

China's strategic approach is perhaps most evident in Africa. China has invested in technology, digital infrastructure and services on the continent. The prevalence of mobile phone ownership and usage – Chinese companies command around 50 per cent of Africa's mobile phone market – will facilitate access to e-CNY money via digital wallets. Current payment platforms provided by the Chinese company Alipay will enable rapid transition to payments in e-CNY. Huawei provides 70 per cent of Africa's network coverage. Moreover, e-CNY's availability also off-line will be a further selling point, through the use of the Bluetooth-certificated Huawei mobile phone "MATE 40 pro". More generally the deployment of e-CNY would enable the expansion of intra-African and Africa–China trade flows, overcoming the issues that have beset previous currency union attempts in regions of Africa to stimulate trade flows.

These initiatives are regarded by US commentators as China's attempt to use the e-CNY, linked to a China-dominated "blockchain infrastructure", to cement and protect its BRI trade routes, projecting "Beijing's economic influence and soft power around the world" and further, that "[w]hile development in blockchain and cryptocurrency is inherently global and generally aligns with fundamental free enterprise and democratic values, the state-sponsored, monopolistic control of the technologies presents a dangerous threat to those values" (Murray 2021). These objections should also be understood as being rooted in ideological opposition to China rather than economic, trade and technology competition.

China's defensive actions were evident in the arena of cross-border payments, before the development of the e-CNY. In 2015 China launched CIPS, a cross-border inter-bank payment and settlement system, and in 2021 (Lee 2022) China announced that it was establishing a joint venture between CIPS and SWIFT (Reuters 2021). This joint venture is a defensive move to ameliorate action by the US administration to apply financial sanctions via the US dollar denominated SWIFT. It should be noted that although only 40 per cent of payments made through SWIFT are in US dollars, this proportion affords the US some influence on the use of SWIFT in imposing financial sanctions on countries with whom it has a dispute, such as Iran in 2018 (and, of course, Russia in 2022), when some Iranian banks were denied access to SWIFT (Aljazeera 2018). In early 2022 (Devonshire-Ellis 2022) China and Russia announced an agreement to develop joint working of CIPS and the Russian equivalent system SPFS. Both of these moves are defensive in nature, even though they may also be seen in the context of a changing financial payments world order.

China also needs to be considered in its Asia-Pacific context. A recent, 2022 ASEAN+3 Macroeconomic Research Office report (AMRO 2022) produced a valuable analytical survey of the numerous projects across the territory. Ten countries are involved in CBDC projects at various stages of evolution: ten retail CBDC and six wholesale CBDC projects, with some of the latter being collaborative. The common objectives include increasing efficiency, developing robust and secure systems, modernizing and digitalizing efficient cross border transfers, reducing costs and increasing financial inclusion.

The AMRO report's analysis suggests that disintermediation is unlikely to be a problem given CBDCs' likely use for transactional purposes.

> Banks may also face liquidity risks if the migration to CBDCs is sizeable. Consequently, various CBDC designs have tended to focus on its function as a medium of exchange and deliberately discourage its use as a store of value, to safeguard the intermediation role of the banking system. It is one of the primary reasons that most CBDCs are not interest bearing, thus reducing their attractiveness relative to bank deposits.
>
> (AMRO 2022: 7)

CBDC money design will encourage its transactional use. Certainly, at least for the time being, most central banks regard CBDCs as complementing existing payment systems. This means that any adoption of CBDCs are likely be modest in terms of design and gradual in terms of the customer experience, depending on the circumstances. The analysis also suggests that "Going forward, key areas for further investigation that are relevant to the financial systems in the region would include the implications of CBDCs for monetary policy, liquidity management, payment infrastructure, cross-border payments, financial system stability, regulatory changes, and the attendant spill-overs within the region" (AMRO 2022: 14).

The United States

The US position on CBDCs has been decidedly cool. Janet Yellen, the current US Treasury Secretary and Jerome Powell the chair of the Federal Reserve, have offered some circumspect support, but there is considerable caution expressed by the main commercial banking organizations and some of the regional Federal Reserve banks. There has also been a lukewarm response from a number of monetary policy academics. The position is encapsulated in a position paper of the US Bank Policy Institute (BPI):

> A CBDC could come with benefits, potentially including a more efficient payments system and financial inclusion. This note includes a discussion of those benefits, and how they vary based on program design. Notably, many discussions of CBDCs list a variety of putative benefits, without acknowledging that many of them are mutually

exclusive (because they are predicated on different program designs) or effectively non-existent (because the program design that produces them comes with costs that are for other reasons unbearable). Thus, for example, if one concludes that a decentralized, tokenized system (akin to present-day cash) is a dead option because it would mark the end of governmental actions to prevent money laundering and sanctions evasions, then key benefits of a CBDC – privacy, for example – disappear. As another example, the drag of a CBDC on lending and economic activity could be reduced by capping the amount of CBDC and using intermediaries rather than the central bank to transfer it, but any cap would necessarily reduce a CBDC's benefits for efficiency and financial inclusion. Yet in some analyses, a "greatest hits" approach to CBDC benefits is presented.   (BPI 2021: 2–3)

The BPI, in evidence to the Federal Reserve in 2022 further stated its serious concerns about the introduction of a CBDC in the US: "… a CBDC could present serious risks to financial stability and may provide few, if any, benefits. Furthermore, to the extent a CBDC could produce one or more benefits, those benefits likely could be achieved through less harmful means. Because a CBDC could undermine the commercial banking system in the United States and severely constrict the availability of credit to the economy" (BPI 2022: 11).

US apathy towards CBDCS might be attributable to a number of sources. First, the use of mobile phone technology in the US for making payments is low, especially when compared to China. Second, the US is likely to support the use of stablecoins, with either light regulation or by bringing stablecoin issuing companies within the ambit of regulated banks. A 2022 initiative from a consortium of major US banks (see Chapters 2 and 3) would see the inclusion of stablecoins, together with commercial bank and central bank digital money.

Rather than moving to compete with China in terms of CBDCs, the US is attempting to use its financial and political power to thwart China's attempt to use the development and deployment of e-CNY to consolidate its existing strong trade position, and its political influence. US Senators Marco Rubio (R-FL), Tom Cotton (R-AR) and Mike Braun (R-IN) have introduced the "Defending Americans from Authoritarian Digital Currencies Act". The bill would prohibit app platforms in the United States from using the Chinese digital yuan (e-CNY) or hosting apps that enable transactions using e-CNY (Rubio *et al.* 2022). The US may come to recognize the potential that a digital US dollar would have in developing a substantial digital currency area (DCA). However, both countries are involved with BIS discussions and experiments with CBDCS, especially, cross-border use of CBDCs, so that by 2023 the US may have taken a formal position. Currently, the Federal Reserve supports Project Hamilton, with MIT and the Boston Federal Reserve Bank researching and testing a "FedCoin" concept with supporting database ledger technologies. So far, as indicated in the recent report of work in the project, the use of decentralized DLT has been suggested as inadequate in meeting the conditions in performance and scalability being demanded by the project for CBDC issuance and management (MIT 2022).

EU digital euro: the ECB approach

In October 2020 the ECB published its first report on a possible eurozone-issued CBDC, described the digital euro as being "for use in retail transactions available to the general public – that is, including citizens and non-bank firms – rather than only being available to traditional participants (typically banks) in the large-value payment system managed by the central bank" (ECB 2020b: 6). The ECB decided to launch a two-year investigation phase into a digital euro project starting in October 2021 (Bindseil *et al.* 2021).

There is little doubt as to the commitment of the ECB (Bindseil *et al.* 2021), if not necessarily the EU as a whole, to the development of a digital euro. However, there are many complex choices, monetarily and technologically, before a digital euro is likely to be implemented and this is also likely to be a gradual, staged process, assuming that the innovation receives the assent of both the European Parliament and the European Council of Heads of State. Adoption may also require Treaty amendment.

One key issue, as yet unresolved is the functional scope of a CBDC. It is argued that an excessively narrow scope may make CBDC insufficiently attractive, leading to low demand, and with the potential benefits unachieved. Whereas those supporting the narrow functional scope argue that it will be crucial to avoid significant displacement of commercial bank deposits and other private sector payment systems. A broad scope would place a substantial management burden on the ECB, both in establishing and in maintaining such a system. The ECB's latest position is that:

> Several conclusions emerge from our review of the literature. First, owing to the digital nature of CBDC and resulting accumulation of payment data, privacy is a complex issue that needs to be addressed. Externalities and private sector profit motives suggest that the public sector has a comparative advantage at the provision of privacy in payments. However, a one-size-fits-all solution with fully anonymity (KYC/AML issues aside) need not be optimal because users can also derive benefits from data-sharing. (ECB 2022: 38)

Essentially the aim of a retail CBDC, whether involving the euro or another fiat currency in another jurisdiction, is to create a digital currency as a widely available medium of exchange (and crucially as a trusted unit of account), while not crowding out other private avenues of funding investment. In economic parlance this entails avoiding excessive "network effects".

The European Commission has recently announced (Smith-Meyer 2022, no page) preparation of legislation to consider CBDC issuance in the eurozone. One major institutional response has been (in June 2022) from the European Banking Federation (EBF 2022), which indicates their specific banking concerns:

> It is vital that a CBDE does not undermine the robustness of the financial system. In case a CBDE would provide the public with an alternative to bank deposits, this could challenge banks' intermediation capacity. This, in turn, could deprive banks of an important source of stable funding and therefore reduce their ability to provide credit to the economy, i.e. their capacity to support and finance present and future economic growth and welfare. If the banks' deposit base becomes less stable because of a CBDE, this will impair the funding management and make liquidity planning less predictable. There should be appropriate planning and control over the pace at which funds move towards digital currency in order to avoid disruptions in the business model of banks, which could, ultimately, have repercussions on the level of lending. Furthermore, households and businesses could – even given the existence of deposit insurance and bank resolution frameworks – arguably transfer massively their bank deposits to central bank digital euro in a systemic crisis, increasing the risk of bank runs. To preserve financial stability, if a retail CBDE were to be issued, an indirect model should be used whereby banks have access to the central CBDE infrastructure, but then provide access to retail users via accounts and wallets.
>
> A CBDE should therefore be designed as a means of payment only and its usage as a savings or investment instrument should be disincentivized. This could be ensured, for example, by a cap on a CBDE wallet.
>
> (EBF 2022: 3)

Given the size of the eurozone in terms of trade – and the fact that the single euro payments area (SEPA) extends beyond the eurozone, encompassing 36 European countries – there is potential for a digital euro, retail and wholesale, to become an extensive digital currency area. The extent of such a digital currency area raises the issue of potentially competing cross-border CBDCs.

Competing CBDCs

Some of the aspects of the internationalization of CBDCs are discussed in Bindseil *et al.* (2021), who suggest, *inter alia*, that:

> One might argue that all major currency areas issuing digital currency and making them available for international use is a zero-sum game in the sense that any one currency can only expand its role at the expense of the others. This could create the risk of global competition to promote international use of own currencies. However, competition is useful and can improve the quality and availability of international markets ... however, common rules can and should be agreed to govern this competition and prevent CBDCs destabilizing the international monetary system (such as by increasing the volatility of international capital flows). (2021: 26–7)

There will of course be several barriers to overcome before any international agreement could be reached. Cross-border financial transfers cover several areas, all of which could use CBDCs in the future (for example, the use of credit cards to purchase goods and services at home and abroad, which sometimes need identity checks, remittances between countries from workers abroad, a foreign means of payment being used entirely outside its issuing jurisdiction). The widespread use of private payment systems for relatively small international payments, generally made by using credit cards, with total terminal and processing costs averaging around 4 per cent to merchants, is likely to remain for some time (Merchant Savvy 2020). In the medium term these could be replaced by CBDCs.

The potential proliferation of CBDCs would potentially involve almost 200 monetary jurisdictions around the world. This might lead to CBDCs being considered essential to monetary sovereignty. It is possible that one or more EU member states, who are not currently members of the eurozone may prefer to establish their own CBDC. Alternatively certain jurisdictions may be willing to accept "sharing" a CBDC. Some of the less-developed and emerging market countries are exploring development of their own digital currencies. What is unknown, and has been little discussed until recently (Brooks 2021), is how successful these attempts are likely to be in repelling either a digital US dollar, a digital euro, or in the future a digital yuan? Being a "first mover" may confer an advantage.

Brooks suggests that there are two main issues for these jurisdictions to consider (Brooks 2021: 18–20): first, the strengths or weaknesses of the monetary system in connection with the role of the central bank as "lender of last resort" and of the effectiveness of monetary policy. Second, the potential inverse relationship between the assessed impact – on the quality of monetary policy and of central bank emergency capability – on the probability of being able to retain stable monetary sovereignty. In this context, for the residents of these jurisdictions there may be benefits from having an alternative currency in which to store and transfer wealth, including their own national currency. It is this factor which may account for the current dollarization in some countries. Nonetheless, from a government perspective dollarization, or similarly using the yuan or euro, may hamper long-term financial development (see Bannister *et al.* 2018).

Essentially, the prosperity and economic and monetary stability, derived from the successful macroeconomic foundations built by the state, in any jurisdiction, will determine the strength of its monetary sovereignty. The problem is identifying which of the jurisdictions/countries are the ones most at risk of failing to be able to defend their monetary sovereignty in the coming era of CBDCs. Brooks himself is not certain, stating that: "... those with the most to lose are likely the least susceptible to currency substitution, while those that are most susceptible have relatively less to lose. Perhaps, then, it is the emerging markets in the middle of the monetary sovereignty spectrum – especially those that have been moving toward the stronger end – that should be most vigilant in this regard" (Brooks 2021: 19).

Digital currency areas

An alternative to CBDC competition may be envisaged through the creation of what have been termed digital currency areas (DCAs). DCAs bear some resemblance to optimal currency areas (OCAs) but are different in key respects (see Brunnermeier *et al.* 2019), although they may overlap, as in the case of the eurozone. Beyond the eurozone there exists an area where the euro is used for payments, which might be a candidate for becoming a DCA in future.

As Brunnermeier *et al.* (2019: 19–20) point out:

> Obviously a DCA is very different from an optimal currency area (OCA) as defined in the massive literature ... An OCA is typically characterized by geographic proximity and the ability of participants to dispense of the exchange rate as an adjustment tool. In turn, that implies some commonality of macroeconomic shocks and a sufficient degree of factor mobility.
>
> By contrast, DCAs are held together by digital interconnectedness ... When participants share the same form of currency, whether or not it is denominated in its own unit of account, strong monetary links develop. Price transparency is greater inside the network, price discovery

is easier, and conversion to other payment instruments is less likely and sometimes technically impossible. These monetary links further create an incentive to accumulate balances in the network's currency.

DCAs may lead to increased competition for those emerging market jurisdictions attempting to secure monetary sovereignty by introducing CBDCs. The high prevalence of mobile phone usage across the populations of many developing and emergent market countries renders them more vulnerable to absorption into DCAs, given the importance of mobile technology in operating CBDCs. Those jurisdictions will need to make political decisions as to the costs and benefits of accepting the digital currency of the wider DCA, rather than attempting to maintain monetary control that is more illusory than real in terms of economic benefits. There also needs to be recognition that for a jurisdiction adhering to a DCA, perhaps because of a strong trade relationship, it does not mean the surrender of other aspects of sovereignty. However, serious issues could arise for the efficient operation of the monetary payment and data services within the DCA, if regulatory variation of, say privacy, occurred. This is a point raised by Brunnermeier *et al.* (2019) with reference to the differing regulatory frameworks governing privacy in the EU, the US and China. Privacy is a concern that cuts across jurisdictions, and it will be important that international discussions on the coordinated regulation of CBDCs – whether used for cross-border financial transfers or within jurisdictions – be given a high priority to resolve any privacy concerns.

The increasing regionalization of trade integration and of financial collaboration, exemplified through agreements such as the recently launched RCEP trade agreement (ASEAN 2022) and the ASEAN+3 collaboration, with trade and finance collaboration in South America also likely to intensify further, creates the conditions for further regional DCAs (IDB 2022). An African regional DCA is still some way off, given the failed attempts to establish an OCA among several groups of African nations. The West African states in ECOWAS (Economic Community of West African States) have ambitions for a currency union, but there appear no likely, even medium-term, prospects of achieving this goal (Prasad & Songwe 2021).

The regional dimension of trade and other international links of former colonial powers in the EU, such as France, Spain and Portugal, may provide a broader reach and remit for a digital euro. The extent of the SEPA, which covers 36 countries, is indicative of the wide economic and trading links of the EU, even if it is geopolitically weaker than the US and China.

Brooks raises the issue of competition from DCAs, in terms of countries that have chosen to fix their exchange rates, which obviously has impacts on their monetary policy. As Brooks observes:

Countries that fix their exchange rate to an external anchor give up monetary policy autonomy in exchange for greater macroeconomic stability, assuming a world of relatively free capital mobility. When a government promises parity or convertibility of its currency for a foreign one at a fixed price, it voluntarily subordinates its currency, which no longer sits atop the domestic monetary hierarchy or serves as the ultimate referent unit of account. To defend its policy, the central bank has to stand ready to convert its monetary liabilities into a currency it has no power to produce. Thus, by relinquishing a key policy tool for governing the domestic macroeconomy and subjecting themselves to greater dependence on external monetary decisions, countries that adopt fixed exchange rates forfeit a significant part of their monetary sovereignty. (Brooks 2021: 10)

In most developed countries, such as the UK, given the global prevalence of floating exchange rates, monetary policy is directed specifically at a target inflation rate (and, in case of the US, the employment rate) and any impact of monetary policy on the exchange rate is indirect. Clearly, it is a policy choice of countries to fix their exchange rates and to relinquish substantial control over monetary policy. Whereas if monetary sovereignty is chosen then the exchange rate, and hence balance of trade, may be subject to significant variation and potential currency crises and devaluations. For example, not only has China been reducing its overall dependence of international trade since 2006 (Lloyd & Savic 2021), it has also been managing its exchange rate, linking it loosely to the US dollar, while incrementally moving towards a fully flexible exchange rate regime. China has also gradually been easing its controls on capital movements, and has a low level of foreign currency debt, facilitating monetary control by the PBOC.

The digital yuan's aim is to facilitate Asia-Pacific regional trade. China's involvement with the BIS in the m-Bridge project and its promotion of international telecommunications standards, including on blockchain platforms, demonstrates its desire to collaborate in international settings. It remains to be seen how far its dominant share in macroregional and international trade – notwithstanding its relatively reduced dependence in terms of trade as a proportion of GDP – allied to use of its digital currency, allows the eCNY to develop as an anchor currency in an extended DCA. It will be interesting to discover how many of the developing country and emerging market jurisdictions are willing to become part of a potential Chinese DCA. In this context the concerted central bank push for cross-border wCBDCs may be seen as an embryonic move towards DCAs, although, of course, these may simply remain as an entirely separate future phase of CBDC development, given their geo-economic implications.

Cross-border wCBDC development

The BIS-led initiative aims to ensure that large financial transfers across borders in a multicurrency environment use the fast, low-cost and secure networks that are in the process of being established by central banks, based on multicurrency wCBDCs. However, the issue of ensuring full interoperability across differing database technology platforms remains to be achieved for these systems, as does the need to establish appropriate regulatory and supervisory frameworks. If the US declines to follow this path, then this may create problems for the wide adoption of wholesale CBDCs across the world.

An underlying aim of the work being done by the BIS has been to ensure that potential provision by private stablecoin operators does not threaten regional and global financial stability. Its July 2022 report states:

> This report provides guidance on the application of the principles for financial market infrastructures (PFMI) to stablecoin arrangements (SAs) that are considered systemically important financial market infrastructures (FMIs), including the entities integral to such arrangements. This report is not intended to create additional standards for SAs but rather to provide more clarity to systemically important SAs and relevant authorities as those SAs seek to observe the PFMI. Although this report provides guidance on only a subset of principles, a systemically important SA primarily used for making payments would be expected to observe all of the relevant principles including those principles for which no further guidance is provided in this report. This report also does not cover issues specific to stablecoins denominated in or pegged to a basket of fiat currencies (multicurrency SAs), as they will be covered in future work to consider whether the guidance in this report is sufficient to provide clarity to multicurrency SAs when seeking to observe the PFMI. (BIS 2022a: 4)

Another motivation to develop new channels for cross-border payments has been the decline of "correspondent banking" across countries and its adverse impact on cross-border payments, especially in emerging market and developing countries (Rice *et al.* 2020). The motivation in these countries to explore the possibilities of cross-border payments is evidenced by their willingness to participate in CBDC cross-border projects.

On speed of transfer, it has also been established – in a joint exercise in the UK, using the UK's Faster Payments system in a pilot with the SWIFT international commercial bank network – that cross-border payments can be cleared and settled in a matter of seconds (SWIFT 2020b). Hence, the speed of the financial transfer is no longer a major benefit of new m-CBDC architecture. However, a report published in November 2021 by Oliver Wyman and JP Morgan (Wyman 2021) entitled *Unlocking $120 Billion Value In Cross-border Payments*, recognizes the potential of a central bank digital currency network as an effective blueprint for greater efficiencies that exist in wholesale payments across borders. The report estimates that of the nearly $24 trillion in wholesale payments that move across borders each year, global corporates incur more than $120 billion in transaction costs, excluding potential hidden costs in trapped liquidity and delayed settlements (Ekberg *et al.* 2021: 5).

The use of wholesale CBDCs improves security and economic efficiency (by lowering costs) in cross-border multicurrency payments and protects global financial stability. A set of extensive regional wholesale CBDC structures, in some cases linked to an embryonic development of wider DCAs, could represent a new paradigm for international central bank collaboration, particularly if interoperability across DLTs and blockchains, such as the Overledger Gateway protocol, is possible (Verdian *et al.* 2018).

The shifting balance of global financial reserves suggests that action to internationalize those reserves, rather than rely on central bank swaps, regional reserves and a much-reduced quantity of SDRs, should be considered. The potential development of DCAs would encourage the prospect of a radical approach to the internationalization of reserves, based on a digital currency unit of account.

A global digital reserve currency/unit of account

China's position on the future potential of a global reserve currency, especially as a unit of account was set out by Zhou Xiaochuan, governor of the People's Bank of China, in 2009. In a short BIS paper published in the aftermath of the global financial crisis, Zhou (2009: 1) outlined the rationale for a change to the current system: "The acceptance of credit-based national currencies as major international reserve currencies, as is the case in the current system, is a rare special case in history. The crisis again calls for creative reform of the existing international monetary system towards an international reserve currency with a stable value, rule-based issuance, and manageable supply, so as to achieve the objective of safeguarding global economic and financial stability".

Zhou refers back to Bretton Woods at which the UK's representative John Maynard Keynes proposed an international currency unit of account, based on the value of 30 representative commodities. Similarly Zhou called for "a super-sovereign reserve currency managed by a global institution" which "could be used to both create and control the global liquidity". It is not suggested that the substitution of national physical currencies with digital national currencies will enable the establishment of an accepted global digital unit of account. The problems that prevented Keynes's "International Clearing Union" proposal with its "Bancor" as a global unit of account from being accepted will remain (Cooper 2016). Countries then were unwilling to cede monetary sovereignty. Assessing the technical strengths and weaknesses of Keynes' proposal rather than politically shows what is required of a global reserve unit of account. The key monetary quality possessed by fiat currency, ensuring its validity and trustworthiness, is its acceptance as a unit of account. The core of Keynes' proposal was the creation of a global meta-unit of account, set at an agreed fixed rate in national currencies, which would provide the accounting standard for automatic clearance and settlement, adjusting national debit and credit balances. The record of these accounts, involving accumulations of debit and credit balances, would be kept on an international balance sheet ledger by an organization like the BIS. This is the same procedure, applied to commercial banks credit and debit balances, that is operated now by central banks in the various monetary jurisdictions. The problem, in 1944, was that the balances could be eliminated automatically only if the nations agreed, requiring them to surrender control over their domestic fiscal and monetary policies.

The potential extensive development of large regional/international DCAs, based on both wholesale CBDCs, possibly accompanied by retail CBDCs, across many individual jurisdictions, perhaps represents an evolutionary path towards a global DCA. However, the problems of reaching agreement between several jurisdictions may be impossible in the longer run.

Mark Carney (Carney 2019), former governor of the Bank of England, has called for a "synthetic hegemonic currency" (SHC) made up of a basket of major CBDCs. Carney's proposal was for the SHC to act as a bridge to a multipolar system (his first preference) involving many currencies. He was also concerned about the instability of the international monetary and financial system, and the exacerbating pressures stemming from the role of the dollar. His argument is based on the proposition that "When it comes to the supply of reserve currencies, coordination problems are larger when there are fewer issuers than when there is either a monopoly or many issuers" (Carney 2019: 14). Carney argues that multiple reserve currencies would increase the supply of safe assets and more easily enable a global equilibrium interest rate. It is not clear, however, that any such equilibrium can exist in reality; it is an assumption of some economic models. He suggests that "[w]hile the likelihood of a multipolar IMFS might seem distant at present, technological developments provide the potential for such a world to emerge. Such a platform would be based on the virtual rather than the physical" (Carney 2021: 14). Carney regards the SHC as a transitional phase towards the multipolar system in which the dollar continues to exist, but its deleterious influence in credit markets is dampened by the SHC, with bene-fits for global financial stability and liquidity. There would still be the problem of political feasibility, greater because far more digital currencies and jurisdictions would be involved, multiplying the political difficulty in reaching agreement.

If Carney's second preference for a monopolized system is given primacy then, via a relatively small number of extended DCAs, it would be perhaps polit-ically easier to establish a "federated global monetary system", as a precursor to a single, independent global unit of account and reserve currency. In operational terms, the SHC would be similar to the current SDRs issued by the IMF that are denominated as a basket of central bank currencies. It is not clear how the SHC would differ materially from the SDR; Carney sees the SHC as potentially replacing the US dollar and presumably also the euro as a medium of exchange, rather than as a unit of account. Carney's espousal of the idea suggests that any attempt to move towards a system avoiding the dominance of the US dollar, especially for emerging market countries, would be a step in the right direction. The desirability of moving towards a supra-national currency and global unit of account might gain the support of several international economists, but whether that would extend to the US political and economic establishment is another matter!

Conclusion

The preoccupation of the world with the Covid-19 pandemic during 2020 and 2021 has moved attention away from the fragile and unstable condition of the global financial economy. Some of the impacts of the structural problems of the global financial system may have receded since the 2008 financial crisis, but the danger of global destabilization remains. The potential use of stablecoins for cross-border international payments is a new concern, with likely consequential problems of global financial instability. The weak position of genuine global re-serves (IMF holdings of SDR), as opposed to international ad hoc measures such as bilateral currency swaps and deployment of regional reserves, is a sign of the underlying fragility of the global trading and exchange rate system.

A substantial global shift is underway as economic growth, domestic con-sumption of goods and services, international trade, and capital investment moves significantly eastward to the Asia-Pacific region. The economic weight of this supra-region, its monetary collaboration, including provision of bilateral swap loans, is becoming relevant in global financial terms. The further collabo-ration on digital currencies is lending credence to eventual challenges to the US dollar-based global system. China is working closely, not only with the BIS and the IMF, but is also extremely active in international standards organizations, for instance the ITT telecommunications organization.

In the US, public bodies and the mainstream commercial banking sector are currently being cautious about CBDC development, although there is a CBDC study underway with MIT and the Boston Fed. The US reluctance, at this stage, is despite (although perhaps associated with) the development by private US companies of the major cryptocurrencies and stablecoins. Nonetheless, the executive order recently signed by President Biden (Biden 2022) on the development of digital assets appears to provide some impetus to the pursuance of a CBDC in the US.

The ECB is committed to moving forward rapidly in exploring the potential for both a retail CBDC and a wCBDC for cross-border payments. There is strong central bank interest, manifested in a variety of projects across the world, in using multicurrency, wholesale CBDCs, many under the umbrella of the BIS. Regionally-based, cross-border wCBDCs look to be the way forward over the next few years. It is possible, with existing technology, to facilitate private ultra-fast payments, such as via SWIFT. However, the low cost and security offered by the CBDC approach is likely to prevail in the longer run. Moreover, the CBDC approach also appears better placed to secure greater overall global financial stability. One exciting possibility for the longer term is in reviving the discussion – arising from the potential development of, and cooperation between, supra-regional DCAs, employing wholesale cross-border wholesale CBDCs – of a global digital unit of account for settlement purposes. Such a political initiative may be required, eventually, to remedy the fragile state of an unbalanced and unstable world economy, patched together by a myriad of essentially ad hoc regional central bank swaps and regional reserve lending. Not in the short to medium term, but eventually, as the global financial instabilities perhaps dissolve rigid adherence to immutable national monetary sovereignty, in a rapidly digitizing world.

6
THE FUTURE OF MONEY: THE NEXT DECADE

The nature and use of money in the economy and in society are essential aspects of how we live and work. Mostly, the structures that support the functions of money lie in the background of our lives, and we are largely unaware of the architecture underpinning the fundamental trust on which the provision and use of money depends. The private money in the UK issued by commercial banks, that we use in all our financial transactions, is necessarily anchored by the public guarantee of the Bank of England. This guarantee is only noticeable in a crisis (such as the run on the Northern Rock bank in 2008). The guarantee is necessary because for each loan and matching deposit issued by a commercial bank, there is a matching reserve at the central bank. The public money issued by the central bank in fiat money is the guaranteed numerical unit of account against which all other commodities may be valued. The unit of account is the bedrock of the economy. Whatever changes of the structure of the monetary system, the role of the central bank in providing this essential trust-anchor within monetary jurisdictions is essential to the continuous stability and trustworthiness of money. The lack of a corresponding role at global level is a gap that will eventually need to be filled rather than relying on any one national currency.

The proposed issuance of digital money directly to the general public (and to non-financial businesses) on demand, via retail CBDCs, should increase awareness of the financial and monetary architecture upon which the accepted provision and use of money depends. In the developed economies, the retail CBDC models likely to be adopted may not alter greatly the public's perception of the introduction of digital money as being from the central bank. Insofar as the digital money is likely to be in the "custodianship" of the commercial bank or financial intermediary, then the monetary architecture will remain obscured. Nonetheless, the digital money will be, as is cash, public money, issued with a direct claim on the central bank for its redemption. Indeed, if the indirect retail CBDC model is deployed then this position is further obscured in that the customer of the commercial bank will, as now with private money, have their claim for redemption made on the commercial bank, even though the CBDC digital money will be, strictly, public money.

Digital money, although equivalent to cash is not exactly the same. It cannot be made anonymous, in the way that a banknote may be passed from person to person, being used again and again until it wears out and is withdrawn. Digital money will have to be subject to validation as far as the customer to whom it is issued, and once spent the transaction will have to be recorded as final, to ensure that the digital money amount cannot be spent again.

The retail CBDC digital money issued, and held by citizens and by businesses, is accessible for monetary policy purposes, by the central bank. Therefore, the amount of CBDC money held by the private sector could be restricted as an instrument of monetary/fiscal policy. But this is a highly contentious issue as previously discussed (see Zellweger-Gutknecht 2021).

The indirect model design is considered by some commentators, including the IMF, to not be a CBDC, even though the digital money is issued by the central bank. The intermediation model would, however, cause the least disruption to the contemporary monetary system, as experienced by commercial bank customers.

Central banks are likely to want to continue to preserve the current central bank/commercial bank model, not least because it maintains the decentralized business loan allocation and avoids disintermediation. To this end it seems unlikely that any CBDC issued will carry interest, and the public digital money would likely be used for transactional purposes rather than as a store of value. Moreover, the amount of CBDC issues in any given period is not likely to be large. Central banks appear committed to the continuance of cash issuance, although its use may continue to decline.

For most central banks any issuance of retail CBDCs for domestic transactional purposes – as with the extended use of wholesale CBDCs for cross-border financial transfers – will be to maintain the trust-anchor position of fiat/sovereign money in the economy. A radical proposal from some US major banks for a system – a regulated liabilities network, that would bring together private money, including stablecoins, and public (central bank) money – would create a new concept of sovereign money.

What will transpire in terms of the issuance of retail CBDCs is yet unclear. Commitment and progress are variable across central banks. On the other hand, the development and piloting of wholesale CBDCs in cross-border financial transfer environments, with the utilization of distributed ledger technology, appears poised for an acceleration into the implementation phase in many regions. This development is unlikely to impact on the majority of the public. The central banks, commercial banks, and financial asset management institutions will be the main participants and partners.

Money in the digital age

There is a need for greater public awareness and understanding of the part played in the economy and in society by money as a unit of account and the part played by central banks in the security and stability of a modern monetary system. The advent of CBDCs, directly or indirectly, represents a significant cultural change, both in the nature of money held by the public and in the role of central banks. There have been many innovations in the past in the monetary architecture. The public has adjusted to them and the associated cultural changes. Between 2007 and 2020 the use of online banking grew from 30 per cent to 76 per cent in the UK. In 2021, online banking penetration stood at 90 per cent (Statistica 2022). In the Nordic countries the adoption was faster. The preferred interface in the UK and in these countries is via smartphone, especially among those below 40 years of age. Central banks should be prepared for an initial slow adaptation, as despite the increasing speed of digital innovation and its acceptance, especially among the younger segments of populations, previous changes may not have provided a template. The major challenge will be for commercial banks and related to the issuance and management of retail CBDCs. Given the likely initial choices of retail CBDC designs, some protection will be afforded to the incumbent commercial banks in terms of their loan-creation credit function. However, if stablecoins are lightly regulated, compared to commercial banks, there would be an opportunity for stablecoin issuers to become "narrow banks" (see Liao & Caramichael 2022) and compete in terms of payments transactions.[1]

The challenge is how far to go in co-locating stablecoins within commercial bank structures or to permit a similarly regulated set of stablecoin issuers to be established, providing effectively a new, powerful cohort of challenger banks. Even then it is not clear that such a new competitive cohort would wish to engage in all the activities pursued by commercial banks. It may be that their preference would be to set up as narrow banks. This, according to Liao and Caramichael (2022), may create a problem for the US, although the reasons for concern are unclear. The nature and level of regulation applied to stablecoin issuers (and crypto-asset exchanges) is currently unresolved in several countries. It is possible, for instance, that stablecoins may be reserved for financial transfers within large transnational corporates. Stablecoins are already operating in this market segment. However, it seems unlikely that stablecoin issuers will abandon the wider payments market, assuming profit margins are sufficient and regulatory control is permissive.

---

1. A useful survey of the potential for future monetary system development is provided in Section 3 of the BIS Annual Economic Report, published in June 2022 (BIS 2022b).

Reforming domestic monetary systems

The key role played by central banks of issuing fiat currency as a universally accepted unit of account, explains central banks considering the use of wCBDCs for cross-border financial transfers. Currently, the monetary architecture supporting domestic monetary systems demonstrates active coexistence between the central bank and a relatively small number of commercial banks. The private retail money created by the commercial banks (some 97 per cent of the total money created in the UK) is reflected in monetary-system terms as public money in the central bank, supported by the wholesale clearance and final settlement system provided by the central bank. The alteration in the monetary system introduced by the issuance of retail CBDCs will simply be that the central bank public money will be transmitted directly to the general public on demand, save only in the case of a so-called "indirect" retail CBDC model design, though even here it represents a change in the structure of the accounts at commercial banks. The central bank, in this model, would be directly issuing public money to the banks likely for transactional purposes.

The issuance of retail CBDCs to a strictly-regulated stablecoin issuing sector, similar to commercial banks – as suggested in the US President's Working Group Report in 2021 – would be likely to engender strong competition for commercial banks. A newly competitive environment would also be possible were there to be lighter regulation on stablecoin issuers leading to their becoming "narrow banks", avoiding credit creation (Narrow Banking 2018). How far this competition would prevail is questionable. In the UK, threats to the commercial banking sector have, historically, been met with takeovers and mergers (see Lloyd 2021). The outcome therefore may be a further development of the current oligopolistic structure.

The choice of technology by central banks to implement digital money issuance to non-financial corporates and individual citizens is currently unresolved. Indeed, there are some commentators and public institutions that are unconvinced that such issuance is even necessary (House of Lords 2022). Assuming that it is eventually the case that central banks in the majority of jurisdictions do issue relatively limited amounts of retail digital money, probably not interest-bearing, then it should not necessarily be assumed that there will be the systemic deployment by the central banks of distributed ledger technology for this purpose. If this were to be the case then there will be a need to meet several requirements, especially of scalability, privacy, resilience and auditing. There may be advantages for central banks in using DLT, separately from commercial banks, who may themselves wish to employ DLT. As indicated, there is a role for DLT in wholesale CBDCs used in the cross-border environment. It is also the case that DLT could be used by central banks for retail CBDCs. The model design here would likely use DLT in the lower, non-public, wholesale layer of a retail CBDC, operated by the central bank. An API would be used to separate the DLT layer used by the central bank and the public interface.

The role of distributed ledger technology

Currently, central banks use centralized ledgers, providing a complete overview of wholesale transactions, demands for which they receive from commercial banks for clearance and settlement, using the movement of reserves to do so. Given the crucial role of trust in the monetary system allocated to central banks, having centralized control of the ledger is a convenient and reasonably secure way of maintaining that trust-anchor role. An attendant danger, however, is the potential for there being a vulnerable single point of failure. Failure could occur from accidents and from malicious cyber-attacks. A distributed ledger system for CBDCs may be adopted not least to avoid this issue. It can be programmed to provide a complete record of all transactions across all participants in the distributed network, with identical copies distributed over all participants at all locations. A distributed ledger is also able to programme "smart contracts", which are stored on the ledger and automatically executed when predetermined terms and conditions are met. The synchronous updating of the shared ledger is achieved cryptographically, via a consensus algorithm that ensures secure and rapid updating. This model is being tested extensively in the cross-border whole-sale CBDC projects, including those involving the BIS (Helvetia Project 2022).

There is already preliminary investigation and development being undertaken, principally in the private sector, for the future linking of wholesale CBDCs with the cross-border corporate supply chain product payment operations (DvP) and, looking even further forward, to the integration with the development of the Internet of Things (Digital Euro Association 2022).

Notwithstanding these advantages, it is not possible, at least as yet, to se-lect a single omnibus version of a distributed ledger (or blockchain) suitable for central banks to use for establishing CBDCs. Even where wholesale CBDCs are concerned, the distributed ledger will require tailoring to meet the require-ments of the application concerned. For example, in cross-border applications of wholesale CBDCs, the partners/participants will be limited in number and the transaction messaging will be peer-to-peer across nodes, and not, necessar-ily, in blocks. These limitations are to take account of scalability and audit re-porting requirements. For retail CBDC applications there are greater problems of scalability and privacy to be faced.

The temptation for the central banks, in exploring how best to develop and implement retail CBDCs, has been to avoid being driven by the "hype" of new technology, especially innovating DLT. There have been numerous "proofs of concept" projects, before moving to extensive piloting, and, in only a very few cases, implementation. It looks also as if in many cases central banks will opt for the two-layered approach, with an API separating the public interface from the central bank controlled distributed ledger database, whichever variant is selected. Whether the commercial banks and payment service providers will themselves use DLT, rather than a conventional interface for their customers/clients is, as yet, unclear.

Political economy and society

The past seven years has seen the development of new private money channels, especially with the advent of stablecoins, that pose threats, globally and domestically, to public money and the trust-anchor role of central banks. This development and other factors, such as the declining use of cash, have led central banks to explore the potential for their issuance of digital currencies. The innovation goes beyond the issuance of digital currency to non-financial corporations and to individual citizens. This monetary system innovation present opportunities as well as challenges, but a change of this nature and magnitude threatens to be disruptive, unless carefully managed.

There is little doubt that central banks, by their nature naturally cautious and conservative, will wish to avoid any major domestic disruption in the short to medium term. This is likely to mean an initial selection of intermediation or indirect retail CBDC model designs. However, it has been suggested that the possibility exists for using CBDCs to target individual consumer spending. As potentially a double-edged sword this would lead central banks to deliver a policy that would effectively be fiscal policy. Such a development may persuade governments to remove central bank independence. This is an area of debate in which the public and parliamentary representatives need to be involved.

A perhaps more immediately relevant issue is the choice of the private and public money channels by corporates, financial and non-financial, for digitization and DLT in the areas of payment transfer, securities trading and the Internet of Things, especially across borders. The activity of central banks in exploring the use of CBDC for cross-border transfers is evidence of the concern about increasing private stablecoin usage in these areas and the potential for global financial instability. In practice, there is likely to be a coalescence of activities across the corporate sector and the deployment of cross-border wholesale CBDCs for substantial financial transfers involving commercial banks and other regulated financial companies. The prevalence and stability of the use of stablecoins will depend, crucially, on agreement of global-level regulations across different jurisdictions (IRSG 2022).

Central banks have moved quickly to respond to the financial and monetary digital innovation from the private sector. They will need to maintain the same rate of response in future. Nonetheless, the challenges of utilizing DLT in relation to CBDCs has also seen many welcome and successful public/private collaborations in the pilot projects being undertaken. The missing element is the involvement of the public in a political debate about CBDCs, stablecoins and the choices they present. Little has been written on the likely public response in jurisdictions where the launching of retail CBDCs has either happened or is planned. So far the discussion has been confined mainly, except for esoteric social media blogs, between technocrats and within central banks and governments. The ECB did launch a not wholly representative (on their own admission) public opinion survey in 2021. The principle concern expressed, perhaps not surprisingly, was about privacy. Another problem was that the explanation of CBDC issuance, and hence the general public's understanding, was limited. This problem is also why the testing of use-cases may also be of limited value unless the full modalities of specific CBDCs are explained to potential users.

The evidence, from previous historical innovations, including digitization, is that the public do become familiar and accustomed to working with changes in monetary system and banking structures and modes of operation. However, as might be expected, the assimilation of the changes tends to happen over a number of years. Two groups are important not to neglect in the process: the older generations and those financially excluded because of low income and education status. The excluded segment of the population, often unbanked, may well benefit from the introduction of retail CBDCs, dependent on which model design is implemented. Moreover, cash seems unlikely to disappear any time soon, which will be a relief to a relatively large section of populations.

A global perspective

As described in Chapter 5, the potential advent of the use of wholesale CBDCs in cross-border financial product transfers in an international context is occurring at a time of systemic financial instability and fragility, and of tremendous geo-economic and geopolitical change. Trade, consumption, and financial power is moving eastward to the Asia-Pacific supra-region. The fact that China, followed by several Asian jurisdictions and encouraged also by ASEAN, has been a leader in the development of CBDCs is testament to this trend. In this supra-region, and relevant also to the eurozone, there is the potential for the evolution of a large digital currency area (DCA). The use of one or a few dominant currencies extending across several jurisdictions in supra-regions, and in the case of China, beyond into Africa and the Middle East, is a real possibility.

These two prospective DCAs alone would cover a considerable number of the significant jurisdictions across the world. A similar case could be made for the extended US dollar to create a digital dollar DCA, assuming there is a political desire on the part of the US to do so. Nonetheless, this prospective development of extended, large DCAs is still well into the future.

The clear potential of cross-border transfers using wholesale CBDCs raises questions of regulatory standards, covering both the financial transactions and the technologies involved, particularly DLT. The need to set regulatory standards governing these international transfers – covering both FX transactions and securities – has recently (July 2022) been raised by a new group based in the City of London, the International Regulatory Strategy Group (IRSG). Their report suggests several proposals for how work might begin on establishing international standards (IRSG 2022).

There will, undoubtedly, be a negative reaction from the US to the prospect of large DCAs, and probably pressure against such a development. However, the US dollar is used as the main currency in 13 jurisdictions, and 10 more where it is a significant secondary currency. Many of these jurisdictions would qualify as being in a US supra-region. This ignores the fact that the US dollar is already the largest global reserve currency, accounting for 60 per cent of the foreign currency reserves of all central banks. Obviously, the dominant position of the US stems from the Bretton Woods conference. However, as Chapter 5 recounts, the latest IMF statistics show that effective, globally available financial reserves, to be deployed in trade and economic crises, are now dominated by a combination of currency BSLs (most involving the Federal Reserve), regional reserves, and, with a substantial fall in percentage terms from around 90 per cent to around 25 per cent since the 2007/08 financial crisis, IMF special drawing rights. Regional reserves and BSLs now represent 75 per cent of total reserves, with BSLs representing around 45 per cent of the total, with around 30 per cent represented by regional reserves. This is not a stable global position.

The current geopolitical antagonism towards China, whatever, for some, may be its ostensible overall justification, ignores the understandable desire of China to protect its wider financial and economic interests. China holds around 14 per cent of total US dollar reserves held by other countries, only Japan has a higher percentage. China's acknowledged longer-term interests lie in seeing a movement to an independent global unit of account. The US shows no signs of supporting any such move to dislodge the dollar from its dominant global position, with the Federal Reserve providing lender of last resort support – in cooperation with a limited cohort of central banks in five other advanced economies – effectively defending the offshore dollar system.

Chapter 5 suggested that, assuming the eventual launch of a US wholesale CBDC for cross-border financial transfers, it may be possible within the next 20 years, for there to be three globally dominant DCAs, covering the three major supra-regions and their tributary jurisdictions across the world. There will be other DCAs, although the three identified would have to be the prime movers. The stage might then be set for an eventual agreement on an independent global unit of account. If this appears somewhat utopian, and it is certainly very much a future scenario for a variety of reasons, intensifying global cooperation will have to occur to deal with climate change. A similar collaboration will be required, eventually, to establish a stable global financial and monetary architecture, an argument deployed by Mark Carney (Carney 2019).

The monetary system reform being discussed is significant and should not be undertaken without a wide, informed public debate. In an increasingly technocratic age, change can be disruptive, even when there are net benefits. Clear, honest messaging about the actions to be taken is imperative. There will need to be discussions in parliaments, consultations with civil society organizations, notably business (including, obviously, financial institutions), trade unions, consumer groups, and others representing segments of society. Consulting the public through surveys or citizen assemblies will be necessary. Essentially, the fullest possible public consultation should be carried out before governments and central banks decide whether or not to proceed to introduce retail CBDCs.

It will be important to monitor future implementation and to be vigilant about evolutionary changes. A permanent independent body with oversight of the implementation of CBDCs, reporting to parliaments, maybe be prudent. Wholesale CBDCs will be less of a concern for the general public, although parliamentary and civil society group consultation will be required here also.

It is clear in both domestic and international contexts that the introduction of central bank digital currencies, domestic retail and wholesale cross-border, is one the world has to contemplate. The future role of sovereign central bank fiat currencies is being challenged by currently unregulated, private money channels. The role of international organizations such as the G20, the BIS, the IMF, and the responses of civil society organizations, will be important in resolving the issues involved at global level.

Manifestly too, will be the attitude and responses of the various populations, as they experience the spread of digitization to the financial and monetary economic systems, within which they lead their daily lives. Notwithstanding the technocratic nature of the proposed development of a new form of digital money, any such change represents a cultural innovation affecting all citizens and requires the widest possible public discussion of the issues involved.

APPENDIX 1
RETAIL CBDC CASE STUDIES

China

China's interest in potentially establishing a CBDC began in 2014 when a study of retail digital money was initiated by the People's Bank of China (Higgins 2016). In 2017, China's State Council approved the PBOC's proposal, in cooperation with commercial banks, to design the CBDC. This work was done by a Digital Currency Research Institute under the aegis of the PBOC and its aim is to design a digital currency electronic payment (DCEP) system that will function much like a digital form of cash. For retail payments it will operate principally through smartphones.

At the end of 2017, on the approval of the State Council, the PBOC began to work with commercial institutions in developing and testing digital fiat currency (hereinafter referred to as e-CNY, a provisional abbreviation following international practice). In May 2019, PBOC governor Yi Gang stated that "top-level design" of e-CNY had already been completed and announced that initial pilot projects would take place in Chengdu, Shenzhen, Suzhou and Xiong'an (Lloyd & Savic 2021). In Suzhou, for example, some government workers were told to download an e-CNY digital wallet app. In May 2020, government workers in Suzhou began to be paid portions of a transportation subsidy via DCEP (Fathi 2022).

The general concern for the PBOC, along with other central banks at the time, was that the introduction of a sizeable, global, private payments digital currency, such as Diem, could eventually mean that they might lose control over the issuance of their currency, including cash, as a medium of exchange. China has experienced a substantial move to cashless payments, which has meant that individuals have been losing direct access (because of the increasing dominance of Alipay and Tencent payment applications) to the cash renminbi as China's currency.[1] The introduction of a CBDC would not only resolve this problem, but

---

1. It is worth noting that for, slightly anachronistic historical reasons the renminbi is the currency as a medium of exchange, distinguished from the yuan as the unit of account.

monetary policy could be, if desired, directly transmitted to the general public (BIS 2021).

According to the PBOC's own survey conducted in 2019 (PBOC 2021b), mobile payments accounted for 66 per cent of all transactions and 59 per cent of the total value, whereas those paid in cash accounted for 23 per cent and 16 per cent, and those paid by card 7 per cent and 23 per cent, respectively. Among those surveyed, 46 per cent used no cash in any transaction during the survey period. It should be noted, however, that total cash in circulation (M) has shown a small rise: from RMB6.83 trillion in 2016 to RMB8.43 trillion in 2020. In the areas where financial services are less available, in particular, cash usage is still quite common.

Chinese consumers appear to be readily adopting the e-CNY, given their familiarity with existing private mobile payment platforms, now involved with its distribution. There are now 261 million wallets held (Unlock Media 2022). It only took a few years for mobile payments to go from a novelty to widespread use. Several major companies are also making plans to use the new digital currency. The ride-hailing app Didi Chuxing has entered into a "strategic partnership" (Feng 2020) with the PBOC that could eventually allow its 500-plus million users to pay for rides with e-CNY. US companies operating in China such as McDonalds, Starbucks and Subway are likewise to be included in testing the new digital currency (Graves 2021).

The PBOC describe the e-CNY as being issued by the central bank and operated by authorized operators, namely commercial banks. According to the PBOC, "The digital fiat currency is value-based on the Yuan (unit of account) as a token-based hybrid payment instrument" (see Chapter 2), with legal tender status and "a loosely-coupled account linkage" (PBOC 2021b). The e-CNY represents the central bank's liabilities to the public, backed by sovereign credit. The issuance and circulation of the e-CNY, via commercial banks and other commercial entities, is equivalent to the physical renminbi. The e-CNY adopts a centralized management model and a two-tier operational system. The e-CNY and funds in the electronic account of commercial banks are interoperable, and both constitute cash in circulation (M0).[2] The PBOC argues that the issuance of e-CNY fully meets the public's daily payment needs, further improves the efficiency of the retail payment system, and reduces the cost of retail payment (PBOC 2021b).

The e-CNY follows the principle of "anonymity for small value and traceable for high value" and attaches great importance to protecting personal information and privacy. While meeting the public demand for anonymous small-value

---

2. M0 is defined, in the UK, as notes and coins in circulation + commercial banks operational balances at the Bank of England.

payment services based on the risk features and information processing logic of current electronic payment system, it is necessary to guard against the misuse of e-CNY in illegal and criminal activities, such as tele-fraud, internet gambling, money laundering and tax evasion by making sure that transactions comply with internationally agreed AML/CFT requirements

Although, the e-CNY issuance is technically still in a pilot phase, and has not yet launched nationally, its extensive regional and city piloting has seen, as of 30 June 2021, the e-CNY applied in over 1.32 million scenarios, covering utility payment, catering services, transportation, shopping and government services (PBOC 2021). More than 20,870,000 personal wallets and over 3,500,000 corporate wallets had been opened, with transaction volume totalling 70,750,000 at a value approximating RMB34.5 billion.

During the R&D phase and in the current pilot phase, the PBOC has exchanged views with international organizations such as the Financial Stability Board, the Bank for International Settlements, the International Monetary Fund and the World Bank. The PBOC has also discussed cutting-edge issues on digital fiat currency with monetary and fiscal authorities and regulators in several jurisdictions, multinational financial institutions and top universities. It actively participated in setting standards for digital fiat currency and building an international standard system under the framework of international organizations. The PBOC (Digital Currency Initiative) has signed a Memorandum of Understanding with the Hong Kong Monetary Authority and the BIS CBDC Hub, clearly indicating China's desire to cooperate internationally in the area of CBDC development.

China has also joined the Multiple CBDC Bridge project (m-CBDC Bridge) led by the BIS Innovation Hub (BISIH), where it explores CBDC options in joint efforts with BIS innovation hub centres in the Hong Kong Special Administrative Region, Thailand and the United Arab Emirates, and their respective central banks.

China made the e-CNY available to international visitors to the Winter Olympics in February 2022. To this end it has developed a digital application to convert other currencies into the e-CNY. PBOC officials (Partz 2022) claimed that the 2022 Winter Olympics participants, visitors and organizers may have spent more than $300,000 in China's e-CNY every day. As can be seen, China is well ahead of other central banks in the extensive piloting of the e-CNY as a retail CBDC. Nonetheless, China is also collaborating extensively with the international banking authorities to share its research and practical experience.

Sweden

Sweden is the first EU country to explore the potential for a retail CBDC, experimenting in the initial phase with DLT as a platform on which the CBDC might, in the future, be deployed. In 2019, the Riksbank established the e-krona pilot division, with the task of increasing the Riksbank's knowledge of how a potential e-krona could be designed, by producing proposals for a technical solution and investigating regulatory issues. In February 2020, following a public procurement procedure, the Riksbank signed an agreement with Accenture as supplier of the technical solution. The technical pilot solution that is being developed in a closed test environment is not necessarily the one that the Riksbank will eventually choose for a potential e-krona, nonetheless, the method they have chosen is a concrete solution for analysing the policy, technical, security and legal issues pertaining to a potential e-krona.

The Swedish retail CBDC pilot conclusions are that the overall result confirms that:

> The technical solution that has been tested in the e-krona pilot project has resulted in a network where token-based e-kronor can be used for transactions in accordance with the distribution model used. However, the solution based on distributed digital technology and tokens is a new technology that has not been tested before, and further investigation is needed to see whether it can manage retail payments at the scale and fulfil the requirements of digital central bank money. The potential advantages of the technology with regard to establishing a new parallel system for payments for increased robustness and the alternative possibilities for offline payments offered by the local storage are also areas that need further investigation. (e-Krona Pilot Phase 1: 15)

One objective for the e-krona would be to increase the resilience in the infrastructure for digital payments. The technical solution, based on DLT and tokens, used by the Riksbank project appeared to show that such a parallel infrastructure could function together with the current infrastructure for payments without major disruption. Legally, the Riksbank (the state), as sole issuer of the e-krona, would also be its guarantor, even when there are intermediaries in the system. The technical solution tested in the project successfully performed the authenticity check of tokens by transferring transaction history, which contains information about previous transactions, to the recipient, without revealing personal data, and thereby compromising banking secrecy.

The Riksbank has published (Swedish Riksbank 2022) the results of the second phase of its project in a report that focused on technical and legal solutions;

Phase 2 involved a commercial bank, Handelsbanken, in the e-krona network, enabling a successful test of end-users via Handelsbanken's internal customer account systems. In 2022, Phase 3 will further develop requirements for an issuable e-krona.

The Bahamas

In 2004, the Central Bank of The Bahamas, sought to automate the payments settlements process among clearing banks and invested in the start-up, the Bahamas Interbank Settlement System, a real-time gross settlement (RTGS) system for large-value payments between clearing banks. In 2010 it then promoted efforts to establish the commercial bank-owned Bahamas Automated Clearing House (BACH) for electronic settlement of small-value retail payments. It then began a rigorous process to select a technology solutions provider for the design and implementation of a digital fiat currency for The Bahamas and in March 2019, NZIA Limited was selected as the preferred provider, which brought together the collective know-how and expertise of IBM, a leader in enterprise blockchain, along with Zynesis Pte. Ltd., a Singapore-based software development company specializing in blockchain solutions.

On 27 December 2019 the Exuma pilot launched, with an expansion to the Abaco Islands on 28 February 2020. Given that Exuma comprises Great Exuma and its surrounding cays (islands), the Central Bank considered it best represented the main configuration of the Bahamas, making it the optimal site to begin testing before scaling up operations to the entire country. About 96 per cent of surveyed Exumians own mobile devices, and about 40 per cent used these to pay bills or for online banking transactions (Hartnell 2019). Close to two-thirds of respondents said they were willing to use mobile devices for payments or commercial transactions in the future.

On 20 October 2020 the Central Bank of The Bahamas took its digital currency, the Sand Dollar from pilot to production in a national rollout, making it available to the general public. Public access increased during the first quarter of 2021, as financial institutions continued to integrate the Sand Dollar into their mobile wallet platforms. All authorized wallet providers will offer interoperable Sand Dollar services. This means that both enrolled businesses and individuals are able to send and receive funds with any other digital wallet once the transaction is in Sand Dollars. However, some payment providers have adopted a two-phased approach to product development. This would make the Sand Dollar available within their own networks before such networks are fully interoperable with third-party wallets.

Nigeria

The Central Bank of Nigeria launched the e-Naira on 25 October 2021. According to the Nigerian government, the eNaira is envisaged to bring the following multiple benefits, which are expected to materialize gradually as it becomes more widespread and is supported by a robust regulatory system:

- *Financial inclusion.* For now, the eNaira wallet is provided only to people with bank accounts, but its coverage is expected to eventually expand to anyone with a mobile phone even if they are unbanked. Only 38 million people, or 36 per cent of the adult population, have bank accounts, so allowing access via a mobile phone to eNaira would increase financial inclusion and facilitate more direct and effective implementation of social transfers programmes. It is expected that the move would enable up to 90 per cent of population to use the eNaira.
- *Remittances.* Nigeria is among the key remittance destinations in sub-Saharan Africa, with receipts amounting to $24 billion in 2019. Remittances typically are made through international money transfer operators (e.g., Western Union) with fees ranging 1–5 per cent of the value of the transaction. The eNaira is expected to lower remittance transfer costs.
- *Informal economy.* Nigeria has a large informal economy, accounting for over half of GDP and 80 per cent of employment. The eNaira is account-based, and in principle transactions are fully traceable, unlike token-based crypto-asset transactions. Once the eNaira becomes more widespread and embedded in the economy, it may bring greater transparency to informal payments and strengthen the tax base.

The eNaira is stored in digital wallets and can be used for payment transactions and transfers. However, the central bank imposes strict rights to access the e-Naira. For example, currently only people with a bank verification number can open a wallet, but over time coverage will be expanded to people with registered SIM cards and to those with mobile phones, but no ID numbers, although with tight spending limits.

APPENDIX 2
WHOLESALE CBDC: CROSS-BORDER EXAMPLES

Thailand

In 2018 the Bank of Thailand (BoT) launched its first CBDC project (Bank of Thailand 2019): a proof of concept (Inthanon Project) for a Corda DLT-based project for wholesale domestic and cross-border funds transfer using central bank digital currency. A second project, which will only be discussed here in passing, was for a DLT scripless bond project, an initiative to increase efficiency for saving bond registration and sales processes.

The project reported success in three key areas which demonstrated the potential for a DLT system. Firstly, the system was able to handle both tokenized cash and bonds, that is two separate asset classes. Secondly, it had the ability to create and exchange tokens simultaneously, avoiding the necessity for intermediaries. Thirdly, banks were able to settle in cash tokens around the clock and facilitate business when closed.

Other issues considered provided mixed evidence and a need in some operations to adjust the system functionality. For example, achieving settlement finality, which is a necessary condition of payment systems, including RTGS systems, meant the BoT running a single "notary" node to achieve consensus on the final settlement of transactions.

Another important issue examined was privacy, especially privacy for transactions. Essentially, the Corda "blockchain approach" identifies only a transaction identifier of the tokens exchanged so that the central bank, or other qualified nodal participants (namely banks), are not able to have information on the token amounts, the sender, the recipient or the asset type, only that the token(s) have been spent and the transaction irrevocably concluded.

Resiliency, of both the data involved and the network itself was tested. Although generally, DLT-based systems offer high resilience against data failures at any specific node, because each node can request copies of data from other nodes. In the project, privacy issues meant that this was not permissible. Instead, specific control points were established that automatically saved the relevant transaction data.

In terms of network resilience, it was found that in bilateral transfers, if the notary node failed the specific transaction involved could not be settled, but other nodes worked. In terms of automatic liquidity provision (ALP) – a key component of central bank action to provide liquidity to banks running short of cash reserves in RTGS systems – both the notary node and the separate BoT node were critical in ensuring network resilience, failure of either would be inimical to the adequate functioning of the system. The BoT node provided the liquidity saving mechanism (LSM), to ensure efficient running of RTGS and prevent "gridlock". Hence, if this node failed then the network failed.

Overall, the project provided valuable insights into the technological performance of a DLT structure of a cross-border RTGS system's interoperability with the BoT issuing tokens. However, many issues remain to be resolved, including linkage or interoperability with other national currency payment systems.

Two further project phases will explore the application of DLT for the bond-tokens lifecycle, regulatory requirements related to non-residents, fraud detection and prevention, and the interoperability with the legacy system and other platforms will be experimented on both at domestic and cross-border levels.

Thailand is one of the more active and prolific countries when it comes to exploring CBDCs. Having started with multiple phases of the wCBDC in Project Inthanon, including cross-border CBDC payments with Hong Kong, the BoT has since expanded its exploration by joining the m-CBDC Bridge project.

BIS m-CBDC bridge

The genesis of the BIS Bridge project is related to its own theoretical evaluation of wholesale CBDCs and builds on the progress made by the BoT Inthanon Project, and its extension to Hong Kong via the Inthanon-LionRock project. Its goals are "[t]o design new efficient cross-border payment infrastructure that improves on key pain points, including high cost, low speed, and operational complexities, while ensuring policy, regulatory compliance and privacy are appropriately integrated" (BIS Innovation Hub 2021: 52).

The project will use the Hyperledger Beus DLT platform, as used in the Inthanon-LionRock project, rather than the R3 Corda DLT platform, used in the initial Inthanon platform. It significantly extends the BIS current monitoring involvement in the Inthanon-LionRock project, so it now covers more regional borders, additional currencies and greater diversity in the cross-border business use cases, by the addition of the central banks of China and the United Arab Emirates, and the BIS Integration Hub, thus forming the new m-CBDC Bridge project.

The aim of m-CBDC Bridge is to develop a prototype, going beyond the Inthanon-LionRock project, which has already demonstrated speed, cost and operational efficiencies, and resilience in the context of payment flows in an enlarged, complex, cross-border nexus of countries. Through international central bank collaboration – operating in the context of the G20 mandate – the project will also test the scalability and performance of DLT in handling large transaction volumes with more jurisdictions or currencies added to the platform, including developing detailed risk governance procedures. The technology aspects of this area of development are explained and discussed in Chapter 3. The project has achieved success. According to King & Wood Mallesons (KWM 2022), who acted as lead counsel to the BIS on the project, this "world-first pilot of real-value cross-border transactions on the platform featured over US$12 million issued, over 160 transactions conducted to a value of more than US$22 million and participation from 20 commercial banks, utilizing CDBCs issued by participating central banks".

BIS Project Dunbar

Project Dunbar (MAS 2022) is a "sister" project to the m-CBDC Bridge and is part of the BIS prototyping approach to cross-border payments in multicurrency environments. The countries involved, in addition to the BIS Innovation Hub, are the Reserve Bank of Australia, Bank Negara Malaysia, Monetary Authority of Singapore and South African Reserve Bank.

Led by the Innovation Hub's Singapore Centre, Project Dunbar aims to develop prototype shared platforms for cross-border transactions using multiple CBDCs. These multi-CBDC platforms will allow financial institutions to transact directly with each other in the digital currencies issued by participating central banks, eliminating the need for intermediaries, and cutting the time and cost of transactions. The latest report in March 2022 indicates that although considerable progress has been made there remain problems to be resolved in the "multi-CBDC space". Hence, though multi-CBDC common platforms could make cross-border payments cheaper, faster and safer, the project issued "an open call to the central banking community for collaboration", to further advance the project.

BIS Project Jura

Project Jura (Jura Project 2021) successfully concluded in December 2021, and involved major private corporate partners as well as central banks. Unusually, this project did not employ a "regulatory sandbox",[1] instead the transactions took place under the prevailing legal and regulatory frameworks governing such transactions of France and Switzerland. Final settlement of all over-the-counter (OTC) compliant transactions was accomplished by simultaneous transfers in the RTGS systems and in a digitized asset registry (DAR) on which commercial paper (such as bonds) were registered.

The Corda-based, shared-ledger, technology network (see Chapter 3 for more detail and discussion) facilitated both the issuance of wCBDCs and tokenized commercial paper assets for cross-border settlement between Swiss and French commercial banks. In terms of the settlement nexus, the two Swiss banks (Credit Suisse and UBS) were considered non-residents for the euro wCBDC and the French bank (Natixis) non-resident for the Swiss franc wCBDC. The issuance of the wCBDCs was initiated by the transfer of funds from the banks to the central banks via their respective RTGS systems.

As we have seen in the Corda shared-ledger DLT database, there are a number of participant nodes on the network. Notary nodes (one for each of the Swiss and French central banks) are jointly involved, one for each token asset, so that a transaction can take place. The Corda dual notary node structure allows token assets governed by different subnetworks to be exchanged, without requiring the issuing participants to trust each other or to lose control over their assets in the structure of the system. This operational procedure ensures that delivery of funds occurs if, and only if, the corresponding payment occurs (DvP) and that the final transfer of a payment in one currency occurs if, and only if, the final transfer of a payment in another currency or currencies takes place (PvP). Additionally, as the notary nodes are not allowed to see the transaction details, then a further "observer node", operated by the central banks, is able to monitor the real-time activity of the respective wCBDCs, and reconcile token asset movements across the network.

BIS Project Helvetia

This ambitious project is monitored by the BIS Innovation Hub and involves the Swiss Central Bank (SNB), Citi Bank, Credit Suisse, UBS and the Hypothekarbank, Lenzburg. Phase 2 extended consideration of the practical complexities, legal questions and policy implications of issuing a wCBDC. The project is a multiphase investigation involving these partners and the financial

---

1. A regulatory sandbox is a framework set up by a regulator that allows fintech start-ups and other innovators to conduct live experiments in a controlled environment under a regulator's supervision.

structure operator SIX. The project explores how central banks may support the settlement of securities issued on a DLT platform. The project Phase II report indicated that:

> Project Helvetia Phase II focused on wCBDC. It expanded on the work carried out in Phase I by (i) adding commercial banks to the experiment – Citi, Credit Suisse, Goldman Sachs, Hypothekarbank Lenzburg and UBS; (ii) integrating wCBDC into the core banking systems of the central bank and commercial banks; and (iii) running transactions from end to end. That is, settlement instructions for financial transactions were entered by the commercial banks or the SNB, instructions were matched and subsequently settled in wCBDC with finality on the SDX platform and booked and reconciled in core banking systems.
>
> (Helvetia Project 2022: 8).

There were a number of use-cases, four were transactional, involving the central bank and the commercial banks, and two non-transactional involving the central bank only in terms of integration and control.

The business requirements included: ensuring that the central bank is the sole issuer of wCBDC; that the central bank balance sheet is unaffected by issuance and redemption of wCBDC; that transactions in the central bank reserve balances and the wCBDC have the same value date; that the central bank can control and monitor wCBDC settlement; that remuneration of central bank reserve balances also applies to the wCBDC; and that the issuance of and settlement with wCBDC must be effective and final under the applicable legal framework.

The enabling operational project database structure included the notary node, controlled by SDX, signs and time-stamps all state changes stemming from the transactions on the platform, preventing double-spending and ensuring settlement finality. The notary node is non-validating, that is it does not see the business content of transactions. The observer node, controlled by SDX, collects all relevant transaction data intraday. It can be accessed by the SNB to monitor wCBDC transactions and holdings intraday. The SNB node, controlled by SNB, is the technical issuer of wCBDC. In addition, it may assume the same roles as a commercial bank node. The commercial bank nodes are controlled by the respective institutions and are used to initiate transactions and to store assets (that is tokenized bonds and wCBDC in the experiment). As part of the experiment, banks may also assume the role of an issuer agent (allowed to issue and redeem tokenized securities on SDX) and/or paying agent (allowed to manage the cash distribution for assets) to test the corporate action use-case.

Notwithstanding the success of Phase II of the project, as the project report indicates, there are still issues to resolve:

These include (i) the integration of trading and settlement; (ii) the potential challenges to liquidity management by financial institutions and liquidity provision by central banks when moving to shorter or instant settlement; and (iii) the effect of system and technology changes to the operational reliability, security and resilience of an ecosystem. Clearly, a safe and orderly transition to any prospective tokenized ecosystem would require financial market participants to coordinate and collaborate. Within the realm of their mandates, central banks should be part of this process. (Helvetia Project 2022: 9)

The report also highlights that RTGS systems are evolving and may more easily support the settlement of tokenized assets on DLT platforms, citing the Bank of England's RTGS Renewal Programme (Bank of England 2021d), without necessarily involving CBDCs. The report also considers the possibility of actively supporting the use of privately issued settlement assets, again quoting the Bank of England 2021 RTGS initiative, the Omnibus account system. These privately issued settlement assets that could be tokenized commercial bank private money or, possibly, stable-coins. However, in the case of the latter, there would need to be stricter regulatory control than in the case of central bank money, as a result of the higher credit and liquidity profiles of stablecoin issuers. This situation is also relevant to the discussion in Chapter 2 of the CPMI-IOSCO consultation (2021) on adjustments to the Principles for FMIs to accommodate stablecoin features.

Project Ubin

Project Ubin (Deloitte & MAS 2021) is a collaborative project with the financial industry to explore the use of blockchain and DLT for clearing and settlement of payments and securities. The project does not involve a central bank in the structure of the project. The project is overseen by the Monetary Authority of Singapore (MAS) and its stated aims are to help MAS and the financial services industry better understand the technology and the potential benefits it may bring through practical experimentation with the eventual goal of developing simpler and more efficient alternatives to today's systems based on central bank issued digital tokens.

Project Ubin is a multi-year multi-phase project, with each phase aimed at solving the pressing challenges faced by the financial industry and the blockchain ecosystem. During Phase 1, the MAS electronic payment system (MEPS+) was leveraged to enable real-time fund transfers using DLT. MEPS+ is the RTGS system owned and operated by MAS and is used for the settlement of large value (in Singaporean dollars) interbank funds transfers, Singapore government securities and MAS bills. The Ethereum-based DLT was designed to interface with the existing MEPS+ and RTGS systems, which allowed for a working integrated transfer prototype. It was reported that a digital representation of SGD was successfully produced which can be used for interbank settlements.

Phase 2 was led by MAS and the Association of Banks Singapore (ABS). In addition to the consortium of financial institutions who were involved in the earlier phase, were five tech companies. The journey took 13 weeks, and software prototypes of three different models for decentralized interbank payments and settlements with liquidity savings mechanisms were successfully developed. The prototypes were developed on three DLT platforms: Corda, Hyperledger Fabric and Quorum.

The third phase of Project Ubin involved the collaboration between MAS and the Singapore Exchange to develop delivery versus payment (DvP) capabilities for the settlement of tokenized assets across different blockchain platforms. On completion of the project in November 2018, it was reported (Project Ubin 2018: 6) that DvP settlement finality, inter-ledger interoperability and investor protection can be achieved through specific solutions designed and built on blockchain technology. Under Phase 4, a joint report by MAS, the Bank of Canada (BoC) and the Bank of England (BoE), was published in November 2018 (Bank of England 2018b) which served to provide a valuable initial framework for the global financial community to assess cross-border payments and settlements more thoroughly. The fifth phase resulted in the successful development of the network prototype, announced in November 2019. It was also instrumental in providing technical insights into the blockchain-based multicurrency payments network prototype that was built and its benefit to the financial industry as well as the blockchain ecosystem. The completion of Phase 5, in mid-2021, marked the end of Project Ubin, a five-year journey of practical experimentation on blockchain technology with the industry and understanding how it could be applied to payments and settlements.

The payments network prototype, developed in collaboration with J.P. Morgan and Temasek, will continue to serve as a test network to facilitate collaboration with other central banks and the financial industry for developing next generation cross-border payments infrastructure. Technical specifications for the functionalities and connectivity interfaces of the prototype network have been made publicly available to spur further industry development.

Project Ubin concentrated on developing a distributed ledger-based wholesale CBDC network for commercial banks only, in the absence of a central bank. Consequently, the approach might not find favour with central banks! However, there are certainly technology lessons to be learnt from the project.

REFERENCES

Ali, R. 2018. "Cellular structure for a digital fiat currency". Paper presented at the P2P financial system international workshop, Federal Reserve Bank of Cleveland, 26 July.

Aljazeera 2018. "What SWIFT is and why it matters in the US-Iran spat". 5 November. https://www.aljazeera.com/economy/2018/11/5/what-swift-is-and-why-it-matters-in-the-us-iran-spa.

Allende, M. *et al.* 2022. *LACChain Framework*. IDB Project. https://publications.iadb.org/publications/english/document/LACChain-ID-Framework-A-Set-of-Recommendations-for-Blockchain-Based-Interoperable-Privacy-Preserving-Regulatory-Compliant-Secure-and-Standardized-Digital-Identifiers-Credentials-and-Wallets.pdf.

AMRO 2022. "The ABCs of CBDCs and ASEAN+3 developments". 19 January. https://www.amro-asia.org/the-abcs-of-cbdcs-and-asean3-developments/.

Ashworth, J. & C. Goodhart 2020. "Coronavirus panic fuels a surge in cash demand". Vox. EU. https://cepr.org/voxeu/columns/coronavirus-panic-fuels-surge-cash-demand.

Atkins, P. & K. Noreika 2022. "Regulating stablecoins is none of the Fed's business". *American Banker*, 26 August. https://www.americanbanker.com/opinion/regulating-stablecoins-is-none-of-the-feds-business.

Auer, R. 2020. "CBDCs: an idea whose time has come". Coindesk. https://www.coindesk.com/policy/2020/12/30/cbdcs-an-idea-whose-time-has-come/.

Auer, R. & R. Böhme 2020. "The technology of retail central bank digital currency". *BIS Quarterly Review*, March. https://papers.ssrn.com/sol3/papers.cfm?abstract_id=3561198.

Auer, R. & R. Böhme 2021. "Central bank digital currency: the quest for minimally invasive technology". BIS Working Papers 948, 8 June. https://www.bis.org/publ/work948.pdf.

Auer, R., G. Cornelli & J. Frost 2021. "Central bank digital currencies: taking stock of architectures and technologies". In D. Niepelt (ed.), *Central Bank Digital Currency Considerations, Projects, Outlook*, 155–62. London: CEPR Press.

Baer, G. 2021. "Central bank digital currencies: costs, benefits and major implications for the US economic system". Bank Policy Institute Staff working Paper, 7 April. https://bpi.com/central-bank-digital-currencies-costs-benefits-and-major-implications-for-the-u-s-economic-system/.

Bank of England 2018a. "The Bank of England Act 1998, the Charters of the Bank and related documents". https://www.bankofengland.co.uk/-/media/boe/files/about/legislation/boe-charter.

Bank of England 2018b. "The Bank of Canada, Bank of England, and Monetary Authority of Singapore: emerging opportunities for digital transformation in cross-border payments". 15 November. https://www.bankofengland.co.uk/news/2018/november/boe-boc-mas-joint-report-digital-transformation-in-cross-border-payments.

Bank of England 2020. "Bank digital currency opportunities, challenges and design". Discussion Paper, 12 March. https://www.bankofengland.co.uk/paper/2020/central-bank-digital-currency-opportunities-challenges-and-design-discussion-paper.

Bank of England 2021a. "RTGS Renewal Programme API Update – Autumn 2021". 26 November. https://www.bankofengland.co.uk/-/media/boe/files/payments/rtgs-renewal-programme/rtgs-renewal-api-updates-june2019.pdf?la=en&hash=6C9918476BE80C3D8EAF25B478547F1F25D3AB30.

Bank of England 2021b. "Bank of England publishes policy for omnibus accounts in RTGS". News Release, April 2021. https://www.bankofengland.co.uk/news/2021/april/boe-publishes-policy-for-omnibus-accounts-in-rtgs.

Bank of England 2021c. "New forms of digital money". Discussion Paper, 7 June. https://www.bankofengland.co.uk/paper/2021/new-forms-of-digital-money.

Bank of England 2021d. "RTGS Renewal Programme". Last updated 27 June. https://www.bankofengland.co.uk/payment-and-settlement/rtgs-renewal-programme.

Bank of Thailand 2019. *Inthanon Phase 1 Report*. https://www.bot.or.th/Thai/PaymentSystems/Documents/Inthanon_Phase1_Report.pdf.

Bannister, G., J. Gardberg & J. Turunen 2018. "Dollarization and financial development". IMF Working Paper 18/200, September. Washington, DC: IMF.

Bech, M. & R. Garratt 2017. "Central bank cryptocurrencies". *BIS Quarterly Review*, September. https://www.bis.org/publ/qtrpdf/r_qt1709.pdf.

Beck, T. *et al.* 2022. "Will video kill the radio star? Digitalisation and the future of banking". ESRB: Advisory Scientific Committee Reports 2022/12, 19 January. https://papers.ssrn.com/sol3/papers.cfm?abstract_id=4012413.

Biden, J. 2022. Executive Order on Ensuring Responsible Development of Digital Assets. White House, 9 March. https://www.whitehouse.gov/briefing-room/presidential-actions/2022/03/09/executive-order-on-ensuring-responsible-development-of-digital-assets/.

Bindseil, U. 2020. "Tiered CBDC and the financial system". ECB Working Paper Series 2351, January. https://www.ecb.europa.eu/pub/pdf/scpwps/ecb.wp2351~c8c18bbd60.en.pdf.

Bindseil, U., F. Panetta & F. Terol 2021. "Central bank digital currency: functional scope, pricing and controls". ECB Occasional Paper Series 286, December. https://www.ecb.europa.eu/pub/pdf/scpops/ecb.op286~9d472374ea.en.pdf.

BIS 2003. "The role of central bank money in payment systems." CPMI Papers 55, 12 August. https://www.bis.org/cpmi/publ/d55.pdf.

BIS 2019. "New correspondent banking data: the decline continues". https://www.bis.org/cpmi/paysysinfo/corr_bank_data/corr_bank_data_commentary_1905.htm.

BIS 2020. "Central bank digital currencies: foundational principles and core features". BIS Report 1. https://www.bis.org/publ/othp33.pdf.

BIS 2021. "Central bank digital currencies: executive summary". September. https://www.bis.org/publ/othp42.pdf.

BIS 2022a. "Application of the Principles for Financial Market Structures to stablecoin arrangements". July. https://www.bis.org/cpmi/publ/d206.pdf.

BIS 2022b. *BIS Annual Economic Report 2022*. 26 June. https://www.bis.org/publ/arpdf/ar2022e.htm.

BIS Innovation Hub 2021. "Inthanon-LionRock to m-Bridge". September. https://www.bis.org/publ/othp40.pdf.

Bloomberg Intelligence 2021. "How a digital yuan threatens China banks, Alipay and WeChat Pay". 6 December. https://www.bloomberg.com/professional/blog/how-a-digital-yuan-threatens-china-banks-alipay-and-wechat-pay/.

Bojkova, V. *et al*. 2020. "The ECB's mandate: wider perspectives on European monetary policies". London: Global Policy Institute. https://gpilondon.com/people/posts-viara-bojkova/the-ecbs-mandate-wider-perspectives-on-european-union-monetary-policies.

Bossu, W. *et al*. 2020. "Aspects of central bank digital currency central bank and monetary law considerations". IMF Working Paper No. 2020/254, 20 November. https://www.imf.org/en/Publications/WP/Issues/2020/11/20/Legal--49827.

Brookings Institute 2020. "Design choices for CBDC". Working Paper 140, 23 July. https://www.brookings.edu/wp-content/uploads/2020/07/Design-Choices-for-CBDC_Final-for-web.pdf.

Brooks, S. 2021. "Revisiting the monetary sovereignty rationale for CBDCs". Staff Discussion Papers 2021-17, Bank of Canada, 17 December. https://www.bankofcanada.ca/wp-content/uploads/2021/12/sdp2021-17.pdf.

Brunnermeier, M., H. James & J.-P. Landau 2019. "The digitalization of money". NBER Working Paper No. 26300.

Carney M. 2019. "The growing challenges for monetary policy in the international monetary and financial system". Speech at the Jackson Hole Symposium, 14 August. https://www.bankofengland.co.uk/-/media/boe/files/speech/2019/the-growing-challenges-for-monetary-policy-speech-by-mark-carney.pdf.

CCAF 2021. *The 2nd Global Alternative Finance Benchmarking Report*. June. https://www.jbs.cam.ac.uk/wp-content/uploads/2021/06/ccaf-2021-06-report-2nd-global-alternative-finance-benchmarking-study-report.pdf.

Cecchetti, S. & K. Schoenholtz 2021. "Central bank digital currency: the battle for the soul of the financial system". London: CEPR Press. https://cepr.org/voxeu/columns/central-bank-digital-currency-battle-soul-financial-system.

Chen, S. *et al*. 2021. "CBDCs in emerging market economies". BIS Papers No. 123, 8 April. https://www.bis.org/publ/bppdf/bispap123.pdf.

CPMI 2012. "Principles for financial market structures". CPMI Papers No 101, 12 April. https://www.bis.org/cpmi/publ/d101.htm.

CPMI 2017. "Distributed ledger technology in payment, clearing and settlement: an analytical framework". CPMI Papers No 157, 27 February. https://www.bis.org/cpmi/publ/d157.pdf.

CTFC 2021. "CFTC Press Release Number 8450 – 21". 15 October. https://www.cftc.gov/PressRoom/PressReleases/8450-21.

Cunliffe, J. 2021a. "Do we need 'public money'?" Speech to OMFIF Digital Money Institute, London, 13 May.

Cunliffe, J. 2021b. Oral Evidence to House of Lords Economic Affairs Committee. 23 November. https://committees.parliament.uk/oralevidence/3062/html/.

Daxue Consulting 2022. "Payment methods in China: how China became a mobile-first nation". 3 August. https://daxueconsulting.com/payment-methods-in-china/.

Deloitte & MAS 2021. "Project Ubin Phase 1: SGD on Distributed Ledger". Singapore: Deloitte. https://www.mas.gov.sg/publications/monographs-or-information-paper/2021/project-ubin-phase-1#:~:text=MAS%20partnering%20with%20R3%2C%20a,Bank%20of%20America%20Merrill%20Lynch.

Devonshire-Ellis, C. 2022. "Russia and China to develop SWIFT avoiding international financial systems". Russia Briefing, 11 January. https://www.russia-briefing.com/news/russia-and-china-to-develop-swift-avoiding-international-financial-systems.html/.

DiCaprio, A. & T. McLaughlin 2022. "The regulated liability network on Corda". Blogpost, 4 January. https://www.r3.com/blog/the-regulated-liability-network-on-corda/.

Dodd, N. 2014. *The Social Life of Money*. Princeton, NJ: Princeton University Press.

EBF 2022. "Digital euro: EBF presents its views to ECB". 13 January. https://www.ebf.eu/innovation-cybersecurity/digital-euro-ebf-submits-views-to-ecb/.

ECB 2020a. "Project Stella: balancing confidentiality and auditability in a distributed ledger environment". February. https://www.ecb.europa.eu/paym/intro/publications/pdf/ecb.miptopical200212.en.pdf.

ECB 2020b. "Report on a digital euro". October. https://www.ecb.europa.eu/pub/pdf/other/Report_on_a_digital_euro~4d7268b458.en.pdf.

Eichengreen, B. 2017. "The dollar's days as the world's most important currency are numbered". Quartz interview, 12 November. https://qz.com/1150533/the-dollars-days-as-the-worlds-most-important-currency-are-numbered.

Ekberg, J. *et al.* 2021. "Unlocking $120 billion in cross-border payments". Report for Oliver Wyman and JPMorgan Chase Bank. November. https://www.oliverwyman.com/content/dam/oliverwyman/v2/publications/2021/nov/unlocking-120-billion-value-in-cross-border-payments.pdf.

Engen, J. 2022. "Lesson from a mobile payment revolution". *American Banker* 128(5): 18–21. https://www.americanbanker.com/news/why-chinas-mobile-payments-revolution-matters-for-us-bankers.

Enwood, D. 2021. "Zero-knowledge proofs – a powerful addition to blockchain". Blog post, Blockhead Technologies, 1 June. https://blockheadtechnologies.com/zero-knowledge-proofs-a-powerful-addition-to-blockchain/.

Equifax 2018. "Cybersecurity incident 2017: information for UK consumers". Press release, 20 September. https://www.equifax.co.uk/incident.html.

European Council 2021. "Digital finance package: Council reaches agreement on MiCA and DORA". 4 November. https://www.consilium.europa.eu/en/press/pressreleases/2021/11/24/digital-finance-package-council-reaches-agreement-on-mica-and-dora/.

Fathi, A. 2022. "Digital Yuan expanded to cover public transport tickets". Finance Feeds, 24 August. https://financefeeds.com/digital-yuan-pilot-expanded-to-cover-public-transport-tickets/.

FCA 2021. "Cryptoasset consumer research 2021". Research note, 17 June. https://www.fca.org.uk/publications/research/research-note-cryptoasset-consumer-research-2021.

Feng, C. 2020. "Chinese ride-hailing giant Didi Chuxing loses ground at home under Beijing's wrath, as rivals keep climbing". South China Morning Post, 18 April. https://www.scmp.com/tech/big-tech/article/3174645/chinese-ride-hailing-giant-didi-chuxing-loses-ground-home-under.

Fernandez-Villaverde, J. et al. 2020. "Central bank digital currency: central banking for all?". Vox.EU, 25 April. https://cepr.org/voxeu/columns/central-bank-digital-currency-central-banking-all.

Financial Stability Board (FSB) 2022. "Assessment of risks to financial stability from crypto-assets". Report to G20, 16 February. https://www.fsb.org/wp-content/uploads/P160222.pdf.

Forkast 2021. "Blockchain in Asia, Part 2: China's Ripple effect". News video, 29 June. https://forkast.news/video-audio/part-ii-the-new-silk-road/.

Gayer, A. 1937. The Lessons of Monetary Experience: Essays in Honor of Irving Fisher. New York: Farrar & Rinehart.

Gov.UK Digital Market Place 2021. "Overledger SaaS – DLT/Blockchain Operating System". https://www.digitalmarketplace.service.gov.uk/g-cloud/services/365644127504447.

Graves, S. 2021. "China pushes McDonald's to expand digital yuan scheme before Olympics". De Crypt, 20 October. https://decrypt.co/83878/china-pushes-mcdonalds-expand-digital-yuan-scheme-olympics.

Grym, A. 2020. "Lessons learned from the world's first CBDC". Bank of Finland Economics Review 8: 15.

Hall, M. et al. 2022. The Cash Census: Britain's Relationship with Cash and Digital Payments. RSA Report, March. https://www.thersa.org/globalassets/_foundation/new-site-blocks-and-images/reports/2022/03/the-cash-census-report_v3.pdf.

Handagama, S. 2021. "US stablecoin report gets mixed reviews". Coindesk, 11 May. https://www.coindesk.com/policy/2021/11/05/us-stablecoin-report-gets-mixed-reviews-from-crypto-industry/.

Hartnell, N. 2019. "Exuma 56% 'willing' on mobile payments". The Tribune, 27 December. http://www.tribune242.com/news/2019/dec/27/exuma-56-willing-on-mobile-payments/#:~:text=The%20survey%20of%20519%20residents,pay%20bills%20in%20the%20future.

Hearn, M. & R. Gendal Brown 2019. "Corda: a distributed ledger". 20 August. https://www.corda.net/wp-content/uploads/2019/08/corda-technical-whitepaper-August-29-2019.pdf.

Helvetia Project 2022. Helvetia Phase II: Settling Tokenised Assets in Wholesale CBDC. BIS Report. https://www.bis.org/publ/othp45.htm.

Higgins, S. 2016. "China's central bank discusses digital currency launch". Coindesk, 20 January. https://www.coindesk.com/markets/2016/01/20/chinas-central-bank-discusses-digital-currency-launch/.

House of Lords 2022. "Central bank digital currencies: a solution in search of a problem?" HL Paper 131, 13 January. https://committees.parliament.uk/publications/8443/documents/85604/default/.

Hypebeast 2021. "World Coin wants to give everyone free crypto if they scan their irises". 22 October. https://hypebeast.com/2021/10/worldcoin-free-crypto-iris-scan-universal-basic-income-biometric-data.

IBM 2021a. "Smart contracts defined". https://www.ibm.com/topics/smart-contracts.

IBM 2021b. "HSBC and IBM successfully design and test interoperable multi-ledger central bank digital currency, securities and foreign exchange settlement capability". IBM Newsroom, 16 December. https://newsroom.ibm.com/2021-12-16-HSBC-And-IBM-Successfully-Design-And-Test-Interoperable-Multi-Ledger-Central-Bank-Digital-Currency,-Securities-And-Foreign-Exchange-Settlement-Capability.

IBM 2022. "Creating API definitions". https://www.ibm.com/docs/en/api-connect/5.0.x?topic=designer-creating-api-definitions.

IMF 2021. *Global Financial Stability Report October 2021: COVID-19, Crypto, and Climate: Navigating Challenging Transitions*. Washington, DC: IMF. https://www.imf.org/en/Publications/GFSR/Issues/2021/10/12/global-financial-stability-report-october-2021.

Independent Commission on Banking 2011. Final Report. https://www.gov.uk/independent-commission-on-banking-final-report.pdf.

Ingham, G. 2004. *Nature of Money: New Directions in Political Economy*. Cambridge: Polity.

IRSG 2022. *The Use of Central Bank Digital Currencies (CBDCs) in Wholesale Markets*. London: IRSG. https://www.irsg.co.uk/publications/irsg-report-the-use-of-central-bank-digital-currencies-cbdcs-in-wholesale-markets-2/.

Jagarti, S. 2021. "Stablecoin issuers poised to be banks of the future on road to adoption". Cointelegraph, 26 November. https://cointelegraph.com/news/stablecoin-issuers-poised-to-be-banks-of-the-future-on-road-to-adoption.

James, L. 2021. "Attorney General James ends virtual currency trading platform Bitfinex's illegal activities in New York". Press release, 23 February. https://ag.ny.gov/press-release/2021/attorney-general-james-ends-virtual-currency-trading-platform-bitfinexs-illegal.

Jura Project 2021. "Cross-border settlement using wholesale CBDC". BIS Innovation Hub, 8 December. https://www.bis.org/about/bisih/topics/cbdc/jura.htm.

Kaiko 2021. "Kaiko Research 2021 Year in Review". 22 December. https://blog.kaiko.com/2021-year-in-review-f7839d017401.

Kannengießer, N. *et al.* 2020. "Trade-offs between distributed ledger technology characteristics". *ACM Computing Surveys* 53(2):1–37. https://dl.acm.org/doi/pdf/10.1145/3379463.

Kedem, S. 2021. "Nigeria launches eNaira – Africa's first digital currency". *African Business*, 28 October. https://african.business/2021/10/finance-services/nigeria-gears-up-for-enaira/.

Khor, H. E. 2017. "Chiang Mai Initiative Multilateralization (CMIM): progress and challenges". March 2017. https://www.imf.org/en/news/seminars/conferences/2017/02/23/~/media/4273FB8FD33947568A7F5B15B9036F4C.ashx.

Kosse, A. & I. Mattei 2022. "Results of BIS Survey on central bank digital currencies". BIS Paper 125, May. https://www.bis.org/publ/bppdf/bispap125.pdf.

Kregel, J. 2021. "The economic problem: from barter to commodity money to electronic money". Levy Economics Institute, Working Paper No. 982.

Kudrycki, T. 2020. "Blockchain is the wrong technology choice for delivering Central Bank Digital Currency". E-Currency Net, 24 April. https://www.ecurrency.net/post/blockchain-is-the-wrong-technology-choice-for-delivering-central-bank-digital-currency-cbdc.

Kumhof, M. & C. Noone 2018. "Central bank digital currencies: design principles and balance sheet implications". BoE Staff Working Paper No. 725. https://papers.ssrn.com/sol3/papers.cfm?abstract_id=3180713.

KWM 2022. "KWM advises the Bank for International Settlements on the cross-border CBDC project MBridge pilot". 31 October. https://www.kwm.com/cn/en/about-us/media-center/kwm-advises-the-bank-for-international-settlements.html.

Ledger Insights 2020. "IMF outlines legal issues for central bank digital currencies". 23 November. https://www.ledgerinsights.com/imf-legal-law-central-bank-digital-currencies-cbdc/.

Ledger Insights 2021. "China blockchain-based service network signs with Korean operator Ledger". 1 September. https://www.ledgerinsights.com/china-blockchain-based-service-network-signs-with-korean-operator/.

Lee, L. 2022. "Understanding China's CIPS". Interview with Emily Jin [video], 31 October. https://thechinaproject.com/2022/10/31/cips-vs-chips-chinas-alternative-to-the-u-s-dominated-financial-system-live-with-lizzi-lee/.

Li, J. 2021. "Predicting the demand for central bank digital currency: a structural analysis with survey data." Bank of Canada Staff Working Papers 21–65, December. https://doi.org/10.34989/swp-2021-65.

Liao, G. & J. Caramichael 2022. "Stablecoins: growth potential and impact on banking". Federal Reserve International Finance Discussion Papers 1334. Washington, DC: Federal Reserve. https://doi.org/10.17016/IFDP.2022.1334.

Liao, R. 2022. "Binance gets regulatory nod in France, paving the way for Europe push". TechCrunch, 5 May. https://tcrn.ch/3KJsrMT.

Lloyd, M. 2021. *British Business Banking: The Failure of Finance Provision for SMEs*. Newcastle upon Tyne: Agenda Publishing.

Lloyd, M. & B. Savic 2021. *The Re-Emergence of China: The New Global Era*. Singapore: World Scientific.

Lomax, J. 2021. "HSBC and IBM complete successful token and digital wallet settlement test". *Securities Finance Times*, 17 December. https://www.securitiesfinancetimes.com/securitieslendingnews/industryarticle.php?article_id=225234&navigationaction=industrynews&newssection=industry.

Lucas, P. 2021. "The clearing house, SWIFT, and EBA clearing partner to speed cross-border payments". Digital Transactions, 11 October. https://www.digitaltransactions.net/the-clearing-house-swift-and-eba-clearing-partner-to-speed-cross-border-payments/.

Lyddon, B. 2021. "UK's new payments architecture now to be a bungalow". Finextra blog post, 30 July. https://www.finextra.com/blogposting/20689/uks-new-payments-architecture-now-to-be-a-bungalow.

McDonald, O. 2021. *Cryptocurrencies: Money, Trust and Regulation*. Newcastle upon Tyne: Agenda Publishing.

McGovern, T. 2022. "Binance Statistics 2022: Market Share, Revenue and Profits". Earthweb, 6 August. https://earthweb.com/binance-statistics/.

McLaughlin, T. 2021. "The regulated internet of value". Citi Digital Policy, Strategy and Advisory. https://icg.citi.com/rcs/icgPublic/storage/public/2031240-Regulated-Internet-Value.pdf.

Mehrling, P. 2015. "Elasticity and discipline in the global swap network". Working Paper No. 27. Institute for New Economic Thinking, 12 November. https://www.ineteconomics.org/uploads/papers/WP27-Mehrling.pdf.

Merchant Savvy 2020. "Card processing fees and rates for UK Merchants". https://www.merchantsavvy.co.uk/card-processing-fees/.

Ministry of Foreign Affairs of the People's Republic of China (MFA) 2022. "Reality check: falsehoods in US perceptions of China". 19 June. https://www.mfa.gov.cn/eng/wjbxw/202206/t20220619_10706059.html.

MIT 2022. "MIT experts test technical research for a hypothetical central bank digital currency". MIT news office, 3 February. https://news.mit.edu/2022/digital-currency-fed-boston-0203.

Monetary Authority of Singapore (MAS) 2021. "Dunbar Project: BIS Innovation Hub and central banks of Australia, Malaysia, Singapore and South Africa will test CBDCs for international settlements". 2 September. https://www.mas.gov.sg/news/media-releases/2021/project-dunbar.

Mu, C. 2021. "Progress of research & development of E-CNY in China". PBOC's Digital Currency Institute, July. http://www.pbc.gov.cn/en/3688110/3688172/4157443/4293696/2021071614584691871.pdf.

Murray, R. 2021. "How China seized the initiative on blockchain and digital currency". Foreign Policy Research Institute, 26 May. https://www.fpri.org/article/2021/05/how-china-seized-the-initiative-on-blockchain-and-digital-currency/.

Nabilou, H. 2019. "Central bank digital currencies: preliminary legal observations". *Journal of Banking Regulation*. http://dx.doi.org/10.2139/ssrn.3329993.

Narrow Banking 2018. "A guide to banking reform and full-reserve (narrow) banking". www.narrowbanking.org.

Panetta, F. 2021. "Designing a digital euro for the retail payments landscape of tomorrow". Speech to European Parliament ECON Committee, Brussels, 18 November. https://www.ecb.europa.eu/press/key/date/2021/html/ecb.sp211118~b36013b7c5.en.html.

Parlour, C., R. Uday & J. Walden 2020. "Payment system externalities". *Journal of Finance* 77(2): 1019–53. https://doi.org/10.1111/jofi.13110.

Partz, H. 2022. "Here's how much digital Yuan is being used at the Olympics, according to the PBOC". Cointelegraph News, 16 February. https://cointelegraph.com/news/here-s-how-much-digital-yuan-used-at-olympics-according-to-pboc.

Payment Systems Regulator (PSR) 2020. "New payments system architecture". Last updated 31 December. https://www.psr.org.uk/our-work/new-payments-architecture-npa/.

PBOC 2021a. "The amended Chiang Mai initiative multilateralisation (CMIM) comes into effect 31 March 2021". People's Bank of China press release, 31 March. http://www.pbc.gov.cn/en/3688110/3688172/4157443/4219723/index.html.

PBOC 2021b. "Progress of research and development of E-CNY in China". Working Group on E-CNY Research and Development, July. http://www.pbc.gov.cn/en/36881 10/3688172/4157443/4293696/2021071614584691871.pdf.

Perks, M. *et al.* 2021. "Evolution of bilateral swap lines". IMF Working Paper 210, 6 August. https://doi.org/10.5089/9781513590134.001.

Prasad, E. & V. Songwe 2021. "Monetary meld: a currency union encompassing all of West Africa promises benefits but faces a multitude of obstacles". IMF Finance and Development, June. https://www.imf.org/en/Publications/fandd/issues/2021/06/future-of-west-africa-currency-union-prasad-songwe.

R3 2022a. "The regulated liability network on Corda". R3, 4 January. https://r3.com/blog/the-regulated-liability-network-on-corda/

R3 2022b. "Blockchain in the digital asset ecosystem". R3, January. https://www.r3.com/wp-content/uploads/2022/01/Blockchain_Digital_Asset_Ecosystem_R3_WP.pdf.

Randhawa, D. 2020. *China's Central Bank Digital Currency: Implications for ASEAN*. Policy Report, Rajaratnam School of International Studies. http://hdl.handle.net/11540/13024.

Reuters 2021. "SWIFT sets up JV with China's central bank". Reuters, 4 February. https://www.reuters.com/article/china-swift-pboc-idUSL1N2KA0AK.

Revolut 2020. "What is a prepaid card?" Contributor blog, 4 January. https://blog.revolut.com/a/what-is-a-prepaid-card/.

Rhee, C. *et al.* 2013. "Global and regional safety nets: lessons from Asia and Europe". In C. Rhee & A. Posen (eds), *Responding to Financial Crisis: Lessons from Asia then, the United States and Europe now*, 213–48. Washington, DC: Peterson Institute for International Economics.

Ripple 2021. "Written evidence to House of Lords CBDC enquiry". CDC0034, 25 October. https://committees.parliament.uk/writtenevidence/40345/pdf/.

Roberts, J. & N. Rapp 2017. "Nearly 4 million Bitcoins lost forever, new study says". *Fortune*, 25 November. https://fortune.com/2017/11/25/lost-bitcoins/.

Rowlington, K. & S. McKay 2016. *Financial Inclusion: Annual Monitoring Report*. University of Birmingham. https://www.birmingham.ac.uk/Documents/college-social-sciences/social-policy/CHASM/annual-reports/financial-inclusion-monitoring-report-2016.pdf.

Rubio, M. *et al.* 2022. "Bill introduced to ban use of e-CNY in the US App Stores". Press release, 26 May. https://www.rubio.senate.gov/public/index.cfm/2022/5/rubio-colleagues-introduce-bill-to-ban-app-stores-from-using-chinese-digital-currency-in-the-u-s.

Sandner, P. *et al.* 2020. "The digital programmable ruro, libra and CBDC: implications for European banks". Medium Blog, 30 July. https://philippsandner.medium.com/the-digital-programmable-euro-5c1c0b39ae2c.

Schultze-Kraft, R. 2021. "Understanding the Bitcoin market". Bitcoin Magazine podcast, 20 April. https://www.nasdaq.com/articles/interview%3A-understanding-the-bitcoin-market-with-glassnodes-rafael-schultze-kraft-2021-04.

Smith-Meyer, B. 2022. "Digital euro bill due early 2023". Politico Europe. 9 February. https://www.politico.eu/article/digital-euro-bill-due-early-2023/.

Statistica 2022. "Share of people using online banking in Great Britain 2007–2022". Accessed 27 July. https://www.statista.com/statistics/286273/internet-banking-penetration-in-great-britain/.

Swedish Riksbank 2022. *E-krona Report: E-Krona Pilot Phase 2*. Stockholm: Sveriges Riksbank. https://www.riksbank.se/globalassets/media/rapporter/e-krona/2022/e-krona-pilot-phase-2.pdf

Tonby, O. *et al*. 2019. "The future of Asia: Asia flows and networks are defining the next phase of globalization". Discussion paper, McKinsey Global Institute, September 2019. https://www.mckinsey.com/featured-insights/asia-pacific/the-future-of-asia-asian-flows-and-networks-are-defining-the-next-phase-of-globalization.

Triple A. 2022. "Cryptocurrency across the world". https://triple-a.io/crypto-ownership-data/. Accessed 24 October 2022.

Unlock Media 2022. "China's CBDC grows to 261 million unique users". 21 January.

US Bank Policy Institute 2022. "BPI responds to Federal Reserve discussion paper on the potential for a U.S. CBDC". 20 May. https://bpi.com/bpi-files-comments-in-response-to-federal-reserve-cbdc-discussion-paper.

US House of Representatives Financial Services Committee 2022. "Digital Assets and the Future of Finance: The President's Working Group on Financial Markets' Report on Stablecoins". Virtual Hearing.

US Treasury 2021. "President's Working Group on Financial Markets releases report and recommendations on stablecoins". US Treasury press release, 1 November. https://home.treasury.gov/news/press-releases/jy0454.

Verdian, G. *et al*. 2018. Quant Overledger White Paper. 31 January. https://uploads-ssl.webflow.com/6006946fee85fda61f666256/60211c93f1cc59419c779c42_Quant_Overledger_Whitepaper_Sep_2019.pdf

VISA 2022. "Envisioning a future of central bank digital currencies". VISA blog, 13 January. https://usa.visa.com/visa-everywhere/blog/bdp/2022/01/13/envisioning-a-future-1642034573970.html.

Vodrážka, M. T. Bízek & M. Vojta 2021. "Are there relevant reasons to introduce a retail CBDC in the Czech Republic from the perspective of the payment system?" BIS Paper No. 123. https://www.bis.org/publ/bppdf/bispap123_g.pdf.

Vox.eu 2021. "Central bank digital currency: considerations, projects, outlook". Vox.eu, 24 November. https://cepr.org/voxeu/columns/central-bank-digital-currency-considerations-projects-outlook.

Waller, C. 2021. "Reflections on stable coins and payments innovations". Speech by Governor Waller, Financial Stability Conference, Cleveland, Ohio, 17 November. https://www.federalreserve.gov/newsevents/speech/waller20211117a.htm.

World Bank 2021. "Trade as a percentage of GDP: China". World Bank Databank. https://data.worldbank.org/indicator/NE.TRD.GNFS.ZS?locations=CN.

Zelmer, M. & J. Kronick 2021. "Two sides of the same coin: why stablecoins and a central bank digital currency have a future together". Commentary No. 613, CD Howe Institute, Toronto. https://www.cdhowe.org/sites/default/files/2021-12/Commentary_613.pdf.

Zellweger-Gutknecht, C. 2021. "The right and duty of central banks to issue retail digital currency". In D. Niepelt (ed.), *Central Bank Digital Currency: Considerations, Projects, Outlook*, 31–7. London: CEPR Press.

Zhou, X. 2009. "Reform the International Monetary System". *BIS Review*, 23 March. https://www.bis.org/review/r090402c.pdf

Zhou, Z. & V. Choudhary 2022. "Impact of competition from open source software on proprietary software". *Productions and Operations Management* 31(2): 731–42. https://doi.org/10.1111/poms.13575.

INDEX

anonymity   34, 38, 65, 85
AMRO   104, 105
application program interface (API)   52, 59, 66, 67, 85
ASEAN   100
atomic contracts   71
Avant card (digital money)   5

Bank Policy Institute (US)   105, 106
balance sheet for CBDCs   47, 48
Bank of England   42, 85, 88, 89
Bank of International Settlements   4–7
   CBDC projects   6, 7, 136
   CPMI-IOSCO   28, 56, 68
Binance   15
Bretton Woods   98, 114

C6 group of central banks   99
cash decline   19, 37, 38, 39
cash retention   19, 37, 38
Chiang Mai   98, 99
Citibank proposal   28–30
commercial banks (impacts)   75
   business model   75, 76
   maturity transformation   33, 76
   disintermediation   82–4, 92
   final settlement   25, 33
   reactions to CBDC   81–6
competing CBDCs   109
consensus mechanism   53, 54
Corda   61, 70
credit cards   87
cross-border CBDCs   70, 113

current costs   114
   payments   46
Cunliffe, J.   75, 83
custodianship   76

digital currency   19
digital currency areas   110, 111, 112
digital wallets   64, 65, 67
distributed ledger technology (definition)   56
   blockchain   57
   blockchain performance   58, 59
   blockchain service network (China)   96, 97
   decentralized   52
   nodal network   61, 136
   semi-decentralized   53, 61
   interoperability   54, 55, 59

European Banking Association   79, 80
European Central Bank   71, 79
   digital euro   42
e-CNY   67, 129, 130
e-krona   132
Ethereum   70

financial stability   6, 13, 33, 98, 99
Federal Reserve (US)   11, 99, 106
Fed/Now   11

global political economy   96
   regional trade diversification   96

regional reserves   98, 99
  reform of   114, 115, 116
global unit of account   114, 115

Hyperledger   70, 97, 136

International Monetary Fund   43, 98, 100
ISO 20022   89

Kregel, J.   2

legal issues   39–42
liquidity provision   76, 77
liquidity management (DLT)   136

Mastercard   87
MICA (EU)   80
money
  medium of exchange   2, 3, 34, 98
  origin of money   1–3
  private money   2, 3, 23
  public money   2, 3, 23
  store of value   2, 3, 34, 98
  transactional use   82
  wholesale money   17, 18, 19
  unit of account   2, 3, 98
  digital money   4–7
monetary policy   23, 43, 44, 45

narrow banking   37

Omnibus account   88
Overledger   59, 114

payment systems   78–80
PBOC   103, 129
privacy, personal   54, 65, 85, 86
privacy, transactional   85, 86

programmability   62, 63
public consultation   39, 125

Quorum   88

real-time gross settlement system   77, 88
regulation of CBDCs   15, 124
regulatory liability network   28–30
retail CBDCs   68
  direct model   29, 63
  hybrid model   65, 90
  intermediated account model   67, 90
  projects   129
Ripple   47

Single European Payment Area   79, 80, 108
smart contracts   62, 63, 86
socio-economic digitization   91
stablecoins   15, 26, 27, 30, 31, 32, 91
SWIFT   79, 101, 117

telecommunications standards   97, 98
Tether   12
tokens   28, 135, 136

universal public trust in money   4, 91, 119

Visa   87, 88

Waller   30, 31
wholesale CBDCs   6
  cross-border development   113
  projects   135

Zellweger, R.   23, 40, 45
Zhou, X.   103